THEN AND THERE SERIES
GENERAL EDITOR
MARJORIE REEVES, M.A., PH.D.

The Young American Republic

CLORINDA CLARKE

Illustrated from contemporary sources

LONGMAN

LONGMAN GROUP LIMITED
London
Associated companies, branches and representatives throughout the world
© *Longman Group Ltd. 1970*

First published 1970
Third impression 1975

ISBN 0 582 20460 7

Printed in Hong Kong by Sheck Wah Tong Printing Press

For my nephew, William Wallace Wright

Acknowledgements The author and publisher are grateful to the following for
permission to reproduce photographs: Abby Aldrich Rockefeller Folk Art
Collection, page 72; The American Antiquarian Society, pages 19, 22;
Boston Athenaeum, page 86; Bristol Art Gallery, page 46 *left*; Culver Pictures
Incorporated, pages 1, 19, 52 *below*, 91; Ena Collection, Prints Division,
New York Public Library, Astor, Lenox and Tilden Foundations, page 41;
The Free Library of Philadelphia, page 27 *above*; Thomas Gilcrease Institute,
Tulsa, Oklahoma, page 33; The Historical Society of Pennsylvania, pages 49,
96; Independence National Historical Park Collection, pages 46 *right*, 66;
Information Services, University of Virginia, (photograph by Ed Roseberry),
page 94; Andrew Mellon Collection, National Gallery of Art, Washington,
D.C., page 4; The Mount Vernon Ladies' Association, pages 20, 38 *right*;
National Park Service Photo., page 27 *below*; Ohio Historical Society, page 75;
Peabody Museum of Salem, pages 14, 15; The I. N. Phelps Stokes Collection,
Prints Division, The New York Public Library, Astor, Lenox and Tilden
Foundations, page 38 *left*; Prints Division, The New York Public Library,
Astor, Lennox and Tilden Foundations, page 88; Public Archives of Canada,
page 79; Radio Times Hulton Picture Library, page 77; Rare Books Division,
The New York Public Library, Astor, Lennox and Tilden Foundations, page 8;
Roger Butterfield, *The American Past*, Simon and Schuster Incorporated,
page 63; Thomas Jefferson Memorial Foundation, page 92 *above* and *below*;
Virginia Museum of Fine Arts, page 81 *below*.

They would also like to express their gratitude for the photographs on
pages, 69 and 81, which are reproduced by courtesy of Kenneth M. Newman,
The Old Print Shop, New York City, and for those on pages 3, 35, which appear
by courtesy of the Historical Society, New York City; and for the map on page 42
to Henry Hope Reed and the Museum of the City of New York.

Contents

To the Reader

The Young American Republic starts where my first book, *The American Revolution* ended. England and America make peace after eight years of fighting.

It tells the troubles the war-battered country faced; how George Washington and his friends set out to solve them. It shows how good patriots like Hamilton and Jefferson often disagreed on what was best for America. How, determined to make her strong and free, they worked together in spite of these disagreements.

Much had to be left out of a book so small, but I have tried to give you a fair picture of America's early years and the men who founded her.

1 Home at Last

On 19 April 1783, eight years to the day after the Battle of Lexington (the battle that began the American Revolution), George Washington gave his Army great news. A peace treaty between England and America had finally been signed. The war was over. America had won.

British cartoon (1782) 'Reconciliation between Britannia and her daughter America'

When could the soldiers go home? Many wanted to go at once. But the United States had no money to pay them. (In the 1780s it cost more in America to print a dollar bill, than the dollar bill was worth.) Since it was time for Spring planting, most of the farmers left anyway, 'without the settlement of their accounts or a farthing in their pockets'.

George Washington, their general, was not free to go home so soon. It was 25 November before he led his 'ill-clad, and weather-beaten troops' on their last march—into New York City. For the past eight years, New York City had been in British hands. Now, under the terms of the peace treaty it was returned without a fight to America.

After banquets, fireworks and an affectionate farewell to his officers, Washington set out again. He rode to Annapolis, Maryland, where Congress (the American parliament) sat. Congress had fled to Annapolis when an unpaid army near Philadelphia mutinied.

On 23 December George Washington handed his general's commission back to Congress, 'under whose orders', he said, 'I have long acted.'

Hard riding brought Washington home by Christmas Eve, where he longed to be with Martha, his wife, and their grandchildren at Mount Vernon, in Virginia.

After eight years of war, Washington hoped to stay at home, replanting his orchards and gardens, building a greenhouse, laying a flagstone pavement under his wide, white-columned piazza. He wanted to grow old with Martha under 'the shadow of my own vine and figtree', only concerned about family and farms. 'Retiring', he wrote, 'within myself, envious of none, determined to be pleased with all.'

For four years Washington was allowed to remain in his spacious farm on the Potomac River. Not that his countrymen left him alone. Mount Vernon, he said, 'was a well-resorted tavern', where 'any strangers who are going North to South, or South to North', stopped, stayed for dinner, overnight or longer. Eighteen months passed before he could write in his
2   diary: 'Dined only with Mrs Washington'.

TO BE SOLD,
AT PUBLIC AUCTION,

On TUESDAY the Second day of SEPTEMBER next,

THE HUTS lately occupied by the first and third Massachusetts Brigades; the Building called the TEMPLE; and other scattered HUTS in the vicinity. The sales will begin at the Temple at Two o'Clock in the Afternoon.

At the same time and place will be Sold, all the Wood and Timber cut by the troops, and now lying on the lands in and adjoining the late cantonment of the army.

On WEDNESDAY the third day of September next will be Sold at Public AUCTION, at Newburgh, a number of WAGGONS,— a quantity of old public STORES, consisting principally of Horse-Harness, Yokes and Bows, Artificer's Tools and Farming Utensils. The sale to begin at Two o'Clock in the Afternoon.

Only Cash, Bank Notes, Mr. Morris's Notes, Mr. Hillegas's Notes, or Debts contracted in the Quarter-Master's department since the first of January, 1782, will be admitted in payment.

Quarter-Master-General's office,
Newburgh, Aug. 26, 1783.

An Auction Notice—the hard-up American Army sold its military equipment and dismissed its men after the Revolution was over

Above: *General George Washington and his wife and grandchildren, with their Negro servant, William Lee*

Right: *Map 1–In 1784 Washington travelled from Mt. Vernon (1) to Miller's Run (2). Because of Indian unrest he turned back before he could reach his property (3)*

Washington had inherited his estate, Mount Vernon, from his elder brother. He had married a rich widow, and for years had been buying new land both in Virginia and beyond the Appalachian Mountains to the west. In 1783 he owned miles and miles of field and forest. But because he had refused any salary during the Revolution he came home 'with empty pockets' to neglected farms.

He began at once to put his house in order. Every morning he was up at dawn. He rode over his five farms every day, helping to kill hogs and pitch hay. In February he transplanted ivy; in March he put in *hemlocks**; in April he sowed holly berries. Underbrush was cleared and red honeysuckle planted round the white columns of his house.

4

*Words printed in *italics* in the text are explained in the Glossary, see p. 99.

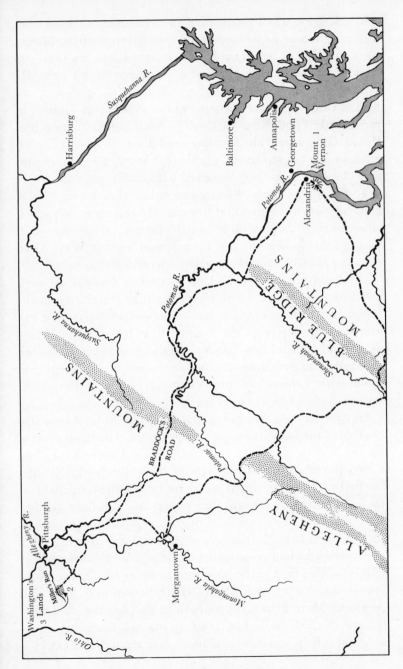

Washington was a progressive and imaginative farmer. (All through the war he had asked for weekly reports from Mount Vernon.) He experimented in new crops and six-year *crop rotation*. He tested new kinds of carrots, wheat and corn. He ran a mill and a fishery.

Gifts came from everywhere: grape vines from France; a jackass from the King of Spain—Washington named him Royal Gift; a marble fireplace and vases from an English admirer. He bought books, mostly on history, travel and farming. His wine cellar was restocked with claret and madeira.

In September 1784 Washington visited the 30,000 acres of land he owned on the Ohio frontier. He rode over 600 miles, often on roads he had built himself, twenty years before, as a young army officer in the French and Indian War. Then rumours of Indians on the warpath turned him back.

While on his journey, he kept a constant lookout for west-ward-running rivers. These rivers might be links between the Potomac River in Virginia and some *navigable* river that ran into the Ohio River on the frontier, links between the eastern States and the wild new frontier. Washington knew that unless the American government soon found some way of keeping in touch with, helping and protecting the frontier settlers, their loyalty couldn't be counted on.

During the trip Washington learned for himself how discontented the frontier people were with the American government. They were under constant Indian attack. Spain had closed the Mississippi River against them. England, although she had promised in the peace treaty to give them up, held on to five armed forts below the American-Canadian border. And as the settlers saw it, Congress was doing nothing to protect them from the dangers to the West and North.

Although he had growing debts, George Washington was as happy at this time as he was ever to be again, 'living as an honest man on my own farm'. His expenses were huge and constant. More than 240 people lived and worked, and were fed and clothed, on his five farms. In one year alone his household, farm help and guests ate more than eight tons of pork!

Then in 1785 there was a great depression. Exports dropped. Farm wages dropped. In Virginia a long, wet, cold winter was followed by a drought and a pest that devoured the grass and corn. On 1 January 1786 Washington had only £86 left in cash. He tried to sell some of his land, but could find no buyers. In 1787 he sadly wrote: 'My estate for the last eleven years has not been able to make ends meet.'

2   A Rage for Land

The young American Republic was very poor. There was a desperate need to make more money and there were two ways of doing it: through cultivating more land and through trading with more countries. In this chapter we shall see how settlers struggled to get more land, and in the next, how trade grew.

During the Revolution the Appalachian Mountains were the western edge of the United States. The peace treaty with England gave America all the land up to the eastern shores of the Mississippi River. This horrified the Indians who had lived

The American Wilderness

and hunted in this great territory for centuries—Indians who had been England's allies against both the French and the Americans.

Congress hoped to raise money by selling this new land—money to pay its debts to the Army and foreign allies.

But many Americans refused to wait either for the peace treaty or for Congress to survey and sell the land before they moved out into it. In a country where there was little money, and that money unsure, land was the most dependable source of wealth. Also, unless a man owned land he often could not vote.

Before the Revolution ended, many people set out on their own, pushing into the wilderness across the Appalachians. They moved into a country of great forests and high *cane-brake*, of rivers alive with ten-pound trout and forty-pound perch, of grape vines a foot thick, and green and gold parakeets wheeling among the trees.

Once across the mountains the settler 'grabbed' whatever land he wanted. He first got 'tomahawk right' by blazing the tree trunks at the edge of the land he intended to make his own. Then by clearing and sowing a few acres he earned 'corn right'. In the middle of these acres he built a one-roomed, earth-floored log cabin for himself and his family. He could stay in this cabin only during the cold months. When warm weather came and the Indians started their attacks and raids, the settlers fled to the nearest stockade where they had a second little hut to live in.

(There is a phrase still used in America: 'Indian Summer'. It is given to a warm week that is apt to come in November. In this warm week the Indians would resume the raids they had stopped during chilly October.)

Congress in the East was no happier with the lawless western movement than the Indians were. General Washington had wanted the settling done in an orderly way, with his unpaid Army getting first choice. He said the settlers were bandits, 'who would be skimming the cream of the country at the expense of many suffering officers and soldiers who had

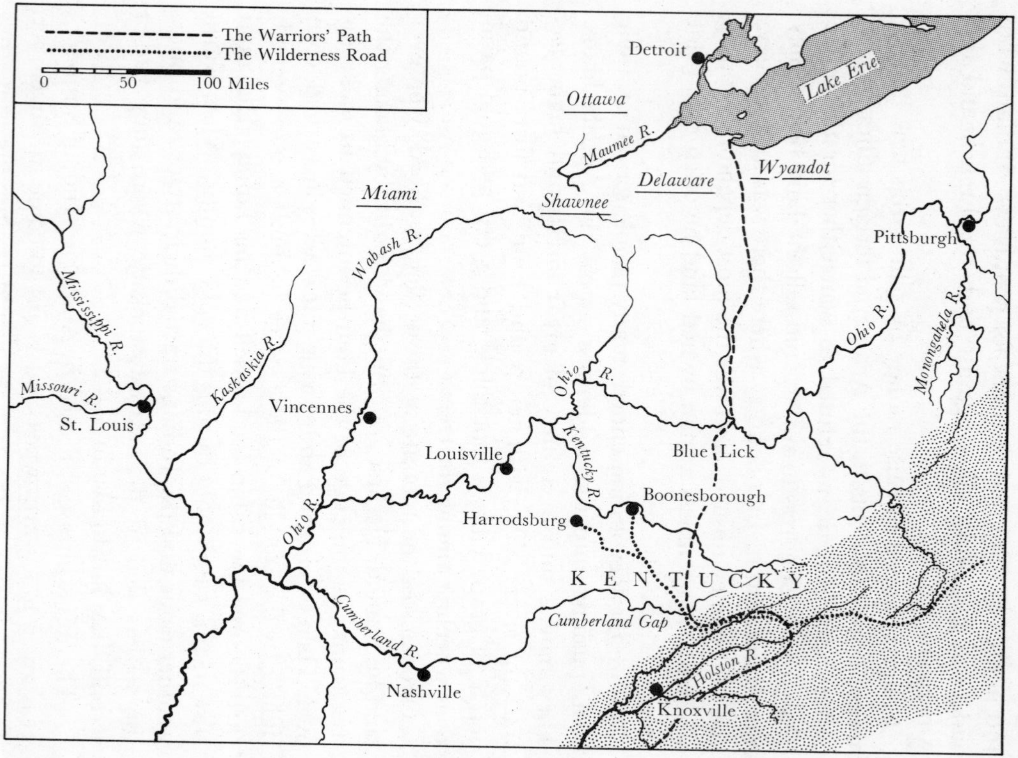

Map 2. The Old Northwest was Indian country. The Wilderness Road (........) led into it. It was crossed by the Warriors' Path (-----)

fought and bled to obtain it'. So the first American military action on the western frontier was not against the Indians. It was against the settlers trespassing Indian territory.

It was of no use. A rage for land gripped America: 'It seems as if people were mad to git afloat on the Ohio.'

If they went west by the Ohio River they went by flatboat. The current was so strong that once on the River, no one could turn back even if he wanted to. On the northern or 'Indian side' of the Ohio River, the Indians lay in hiding, waiting for a flatboat to run aground. Or they would force their white women and children captives to stand on the shore and cry for help. If a pitying settler poled into shore to help them, the Indians sprang out of ambush with axe and tomahawk.

If they went west by land, it often was by the Wilderness Road. The Wilderness Road had originally been an Indian trail through the Appalachian Mountains from Virginia to Kentucky or Tennessee. It meant climbing rocks, crossing wild rapids and scaling cliffs. The Wilderness Road was crossed by another centuries-old Indian trail—the Warriors' Path. The Warriors' Path, which the Indians used, made the settlers' journey much more dangerous.

When it seemed clear to them that the American government back east was not able to keep the frontiersmen and their families from moving into Indian territory, the Indians decided to stop 'land grabbing' by making the settlers' lives so hideous that they would go back east across the mountains of their own free will.

So once the settler had established his 'corn right' and built his cabin, he lived in constant peril. Indian braves stole up to the edge of the clearing at night, waited until dawn and then when the family came out of the cabin, attacked. They seized, tortured and burned the father to death, bashed the baby's head against cabin walls, set fire to the house and crops, and carried the mother and older children into slavery.

The year 1782 (the year before the English-American peace treaty was signed) was known as 'The Year of Sorrows' along the frontier. The winter was so mild that the Indian raids never stopped. From November to May, the skies were blackened by the smoke of smouldering frontier cabins.

The settlers not only lived in day-and-night danger from Indians, but danger from starvation and fatal illness. They were embittered by the neglect of the government back east. They knew what most Congressmen said about them. John Jay had written to John Adams, 'Shall we not fill the wilderness with savages and will they not become more *formidable* than the tawny ones?' (that is, the Indians). Congress was afraid to help the settlers against the Indian tribes. What if Spain or England came to the Indians' aid? Also the five British forts below the Canadian-American border were a constant threat. The Indians could always turn to them for help.

Since Congress did not protect them, the frontiersmen grew to resent any interference from Congress. They said, 'Any fool can put on his pants better than the wise man can do it for him.'

Lack of communication made matters worse. It was so hard to get a message through the wilderness that it took thirty-two days for news of Clark's capture of the frontier town of Vincennes, during the Revolution, to reach Louisville only 100 miles away. No wonder the frontier families felt lonely, neglected and forgotten. No wonder Washington, when he came home from touring his western lands in 1784, wrote of the people who lived there, and their loyalty to the new Republic: 'The touch of a feather would turn them either way.'

3 To Sea for Tea

Like the settlers, sailors and merchants had a hard time after the Revolution was over. The American ships had been busy during the war, as *privateers* preying on the British Navy. Back and forth they had sailed the Atlantic. The same young sea captain who brought the news of the Battle of Lexington to England in 1775 (he raced across the ocean to get there before a British ship could!) carried the first word of the peace treaty back to America in 1783. His name was John Derby and he came from Salem, Massachusetts. His father was one of the richest shipbuilders and merchants in the nation.

But the end of the Revolution threw John Derby and many other American sailors out of work. Before the Revolution, American ships had carried British goods all over the British Empire. During the Revolution, the Derbys, like many other merchants and sea captains, became rich by attacking and capturing British shipping.

As soon as the war was over America expected to re-open her old friendly trade with Britain and her colonies. America had missed the British-made goods, the furniture, clothes, china, and wanted to buy them again. Though the British merchants were happy to sell to Americans, the British government would not allow any British goods to be carried by American ships; or allow any American ships to enter English or colonial harbours. Americans were very hurt and surprised by this British stand.

Months passed. American ships lay idle. American sailors, used to profits and excitement, sulked and rioted in seaport towns. Finally a group of New York City merchants decided 13

A Salem, Mass., wharf at the height of the Old China Trade

to find new markets to replace the old ones they had lost. They refitted a privateer, renamed her 'Empress of China', and on 22 February 1784 (Washington's birthday), sent her sailing off to Canton, China, the tea centre of the world. (Americans still liked tea as much in 1784 as they did before the Boston Tea Party.) The ship's cargo was silver, cotton, lead, and 30 tons of a root called ginseng which the Chinese believed would renew their youth.

The Captain, John Green, carried a letter signed by the President and the Secretary of Congress. It commended him to:

> 'Most Serene, most *Puissant,* High, Illustrious, Noble, Honourable, Venerable, Wise and Prudent Lords, Emperors, Kings, Republicks, Princes, Dukes, Earls, Barons, Lords, Burgomasters, Councillors, as also, Judges, Officers, Justicians, and Regents of all the good cities and places, whether *ecclesiastical* or *secular* who shall see these *patents* or hear them read . . .'

Captain Green stopped at the Cape Verde Islands (where his crew caught a green monkey with a blue face), rounded the Cape of Good Hope passed Java Head and six months later dropped anchor at Whampoa, the harbour of Canton.

Canton Harbour, China, with the foreign flags flying

Canton Harbour was full of foreign ships. The crews—
English, French, Dutch and Danish—came aboard 'Empress
of China'. Captain Green was pleased to report the English
captain had said 'he was glad to see us in this part of the
world'.

In four months Captain Green had sold his cargo and
started home with a load of green and black tea, *nankeens*,
china and silk. By May he was back in New York Harbour.
In a few days his whole cargo was sold for a profit of $30,000—
a 20 per cent profit. Before the end of the year, five more
American ships were sailing off to Canton for tea. The Old
China Trade had begun.

It was a life for only the young and adventurous. The
voyage could last two or three years and be ended by ship-
wreck, storm, *typhoon* or cannibals. Small boats carried boy
crews, commanded by captains in their early twenties. In one
Salem family there were five sea captains, all under twenty-
five.

The Old China Trade soon involved trading-stops all along
the way. As the Emperor of China said, though the Americans
might want Chinese tea and silk, the Chinese had little   15

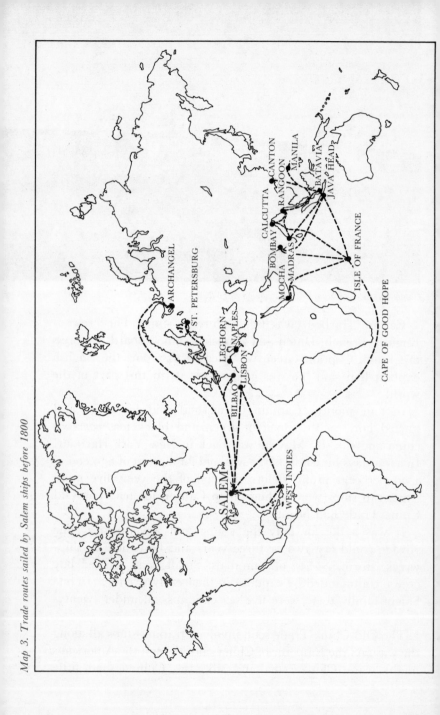

Map 3. *Trade routes sailed by Salem ships before 1800*

interest in America's 'mechanical toys'. So, on the way east, American captains bought goods that their Chinese customers might like. They halted at the Fiji Islands and bribed the natives with whale teeth, calico and looking-glasses, to bring them sandalwood and tortoiseshell for fans; birds' nests and sharks' fins for soup. Then they set sail once more for Canton. Americans also found that Chinese tea could be sold as easily in St Helena, St Petersburg and Genoa as in Salem or New York; that Indian cotton from Calcutta could be exchanged for silks in China.

Soon the Old China Trade included visits to the Pacific Northwest. There, sailors bartered knives, blankets and beads for furs (two green beads for one furskin). When they discovered that Chinese merchants would pay ten times as much for a seal or an otter pelt as an American merchant would, seal and otter were slaughtered in droves on the California coast for the Chinese market. America's world-wide trade grew steadily. All the riches of the Orient were carried on American ships through the seven seas into the harbours on the Atlantic coast.

4   Clouds and Darkness

The traders might be successful, but the young Republic still faced many problems. There was the problem of settlers on the western frontier; there were questions of trade to be settled; above all there was the problem of too little money. A strong central government was needed, but Congress had very little power. During the Revolution the thirteen colonies had come together in a league of friendship under the Articles of Confederation. They had successfully joined to fight and win a war. But once the war was won in 1783, the States returned to fighting among themselves, and the Congress of all the States could not stop them.

They fought over State boundaries: In 1784 Pennsylvania and Connecticut shed blood over the Wyoming Valley. Over trade: a New Jersey farmer who wanted to bring his grain or vegetables to sell in a New York City market, had to pay a tax at the State border. Over money: Congress had been bankrupt since 1780, when inflation made its paper money worthless. A $1,000 continental note was worth one dollar in hard money. (The saying 'not worth a continental' still means in America that something is worthless.) Also, the country was swamped with foreign coins—*ducats, moidores, pieces of eight, doubloons*—causing money mix-ups throughout the thirteen States. The value of a dollar was different everywhere: 8*s* in New York, 6*s* in New England, 7*s* 6*d* in the Middle Atlantic States and 32*s* 6*d* in South Carolina.

The relations between the States and Congress were just as bad. The Articles of Confederation said the States had 'sovereignty, freedom and independence'. This 'sovereignty

Above: *Chart of the many kinds of money used in America at this time*

Below: *By 1785 a bill issued in 1775 was worth nothing*

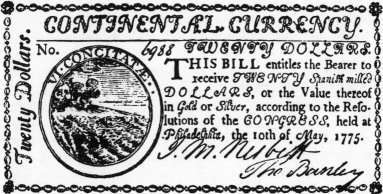

and independence made the States behave as if they thought
they need not obey Congress at all. They refused to let
Congress tax them. So Congress, when the Revolution was
over, owed the Army £5 million and had no money to pay. 19

This is how Mount Vernon looked in 1792. The family are on the lawn

The States also ignored the trade treaties Congress tried to make with foreign countries—and even made treaties of their own. They paid no heed to the treaties Congress made with the Indian tribes and attacked the Indians in spite of them. (Georgia fought and won a private war with the Creek Indians.)

Even the delegates to Congress themselves had so little respect for Congress that they rarely bothered to attend. There were less than twenty men present at Annapolis to accept Washington's resignation, and barely enough to *ratify* the peace treaty ending the war.

The country was in such turmoil that in 1785 George Washington wrote to a friend, 'the wheels of government are clogged. We are descending into a vale of confusion and darkness.' And he and others like him knew well that English forces to the North and Spanish to the South and West were on the watch. If America split from 'one nation today to thirteen tomorrow' she would soon be attacked from Canada or across the Mississippi River.

Washington, James Madison and other prominent Virginians decided that the States should at least try to come to some sort of trade agreements. They called a meeting for September 1786 in Annapolis, Maryland. Only five States bothered to send delegates. But one of the delegates was Alexander Hamilton who had been Washington's secretary during the Revolution. He, as well as Washington, could remember how much the weakness of the Articles of Confederation and the national government had made the Army suffer during the Revolution. Because of this experience, Hamilton was determined to make the new national government strong. He persuaded his fellow delegates to call another meeting. This new meeting was to be in Philadelphia, Pennsylvania, in May. Its purpose, Hamilton said, was to 'revise' the Articles of Confederation.

Everyone wanted Washington to attend the May meeting. He was most unwilling to go back into public life. He wrote to John Jay: 'Having happily assisted in bringing the ship into port, it is not my business to embark again on the sea of troubles.' (He meant that having helped America to win independence, he didn't want to be involved in trying to govern her.) He had rheumatism (so bad, his arm was in a sling); his farms desperately needed his care if they were ever to make money. He was sombrely sure the Philadelphia meeting would be worse attended than the Annapolis meeting. No, he would not go.

Then in January 1787 his mind was changed. It was changed by Shays' Rebellion in Massachusetts, hundreds of miles away.

5 A Soldier's Pay

'A soldier's pay are rags and fame
A wooden leg—a deathless name'

And in the case of many Revolutionary War *veterans*, little
else. To Washington's disgust, his soldiers 'like a sett of
beggars' were turned loose on the world without pay, to
trudge back home to farms that had become debt- and tax-
ridden, ruined by neglect, often burnt black by Indians.

In the northeastern States their plight was particularly bad.
The sea captains and merchants of New England may have
made money out of the Revolution, but the New England
farmers returned to a hopeless life of low prices, high taxes
and worn-out land.

Soldiers coming home from camp

During the war their army uniforms had protected them from debtors' prison. Now when they couldn't pay what they owed, they were flung into jail. Their farms were sold at public auction at one third of their value.

By 1786, when hard times had spread to all of the thirteen States, the farmers of Western Massachusetts exploded into revolt. In January 1787 a crowd of 1,200 desperate men, who had lost their farms and were faced with prison, thrust evergreen twigs into their hats and, led by a Bunker Hill veteran, Daniel Shays, marched on an arsenal in Springfield, Massachusetts. They wanted to capture guns so that they could force the courts that were making judgments against them to close.

General Benjamin Lincoln (the officer who accepted the British surrender at Yorktown) led a band of militia against the farmers. Routed in a blinding snowstorm, the hapless rebels scattered among the icy hills. Shays' Rebellion was over.

News of Shays' Rebellion shocked Washington, Adams and many other recent revolutionaries. Washington wrote of the uprising, 'We are fast verging into *anarchy* and confusion'. Colonel David Humphreys, his former aide, lamented that 'government is *prostrated* in the dust'. General Henry Knox asked, 'What is to give us security against lawless men?'

Only Thomas Jefferson, a *diplomat* in far-off France, approved. 'A little rebellion is now and then a good thing', he wrote, 'the tree of liberty must be refreshed from time to time with the blood of patriots and tyrants.'

Washington was appalled by the news of Shays' Rebellion. He felt his country was in danger from '*combustibles* in every State that a spark might set fire to'. Very unwillingly he agreed to leave Mount Vernon once more for public service. He headed the Virginia delegation to the Philadelphia meeting to 'revise' the Articles of Confederation.

The meeting had been called for 14 May 1787. Washington was there on the 13th. His first act was to visit old Benjamin Franklin in his brickwalled garden. Franklin was almost as 23 worried as Washington. He had written to Jefferson about the forthcoming meeting: 'If it does not do good, it must do harm as it will show we have not wisdom to govern ourselves.'

Washington was on time. Few others were. Only the Virginia and Pennsylvania delegations were at Independence Hall the next day. Almost two weeks passed before twenty-nine more delegates straggled in. By the 25th there was a *quorum*—lawyers, landowners, merchants, teachers, soldiers. Their average age was forty-two. Most had fought in the Revolution, one-sixth were foreign-born.

First among them in respect and popularity stood George Washington. Next came Benjamin Franklin, a feeble eighty-one, but still able 'to tell a story in a style more engaging than anything I ever heard'. There was Virginia's James Madison, and New York's Alexander Hamilton, both short, slender and full of plans for a new kind of state. There was the one-legged Pennsylvania *gallant,* Gouverneur Morris; the haughty South Carolina orator, John Rutledge; Roger Sherman of Massachusetts, once a shoemaker, now a judge.

On 25 May they set to work. They began by asking George Washington to preside.

6 A Hoop for the Barrel

The fifty-five delegates differed in many ways. On one thing they agreed. They must find a way to bind the thirteen States together into one nation. A popular after-dinner toast put it this way, to find 'a hoop for the barrel' of thirteen States, that were in such a danger of falling apart. To many delegates America was in a state of chaos where 'changes will be made by wisdom and agreement, or by force'.

Led by the Virginia delegation, they soon decided it was a waste of time to try to 'revise' the Articles of Confederation. They must build a new kind of government. They also agreed the meetings must be absolutely secret. The only record kept was James Madison's shorthand journal. It was not published until 1840—fifty-three years later. To protect this vital secrecy, all doors and windows of Independence Hall were kept tight shut and sentries posted inside and out. Since it was a swelteringly hot summer, and a new wing was being built on the building, the noise and heat were unbearable.

As presiding officer, Washington sat at a small table on a platform at the end of the long room. There were thirteen more tables—one for the men from each State. The tables were set out from north to south. Maine's table was in the most northern spot; Georgia's in the southerly one, just as the States lay along the seaboard. A heavy green cloth covered each table. (The tables were rented and the owner was afraid they would be scratched.) The green cloth hung to the floor. When later on, the weather got chilly, the delegates tucked the cloth about their knees like blankets.

In the first three days of the convention the Virginians

presented a plan for a new government. For the next three and a half months it was argued, debated and fought over.

The plan suggested a national government like the governments of most of the States. It would have three separate branches; an *executive* (the President); a *legislative* branch (Congress); a *judicial* branch (a Supreme Court and lesser courts). To check and balance out each other's power, the three branches should be independent of each other.

Under the Articles of Confederation all the States, large or small, had one vote each. The large States said this was unfair. Since they represented more people, they should have more votes than the smaller States. The small States—like New Jersey and Maryland—objected. The tall, sharp-tongued Scot, James Wilson of New Jersey asked if 'the United States government was going to be for men or for the imaginary beings called States'.

At last there was a compromise. Congress, like the British Parliament, should have two Houses. To the Upper House (called the Senate, after the Senate of Ancient Rome) would go two delegates from each State, be it large or small. To the Lower House (called the House of Representatives) each State could send one representative for every 40,000 persons. (Five slaves counted as three persons.)

One of the greatest obstacles to agreement on a constitution was slavery. In 1776 the Declaration of Independence had proclaimed 'all men are created free and equal'. How then could the new republic accept slavery? Most northern States wanted slavery abolished. But the way of life for most southern States depended on slavery. Some threatened to leave the union if the Constitution abolished slavery.

When George Mason, although he was a Virginian, denounced the importation of slaves as 'an *infernal* traffic', John Rutledge of South Carolina retorted grimly, that religion and humanity had nothing to do with the question. 'The true question at present is whether the southern States shall or shall not be parties to the Union.'

Above: *Independence Hall in Philadelphia—home of both the Declaration of Independence and the American Constitution*

Below: *Inside Independence Hall—Washington sat at the desk facing the room, between the two fireplaces*

Ruefully the anti-slavery delegates saw this was so. But Mason *predicted* truly when he said, 'Providence punishes national sins by national calamities.' Before a hundred years had passed, a great national calamity, the Civil War, had ripped the United States in two over the question of slavery.

Congress was given all the powers granted by the Articles of Confederation, and many more powers which the States had appropriated to themselves under the weak sway of the Articles. It could now tax the States, make rules for the naturalisation of foreigners, coin money, grant patents and copyrights. It could also borrow money on United States' credit, punish *counterfeiters*, establish post offices and post roads, set up courts, raise an army and navy, call out the militia and, most important, 'make all laws that shall be necessary and proper for carrying into execution the fore-going powers'. The new constitution also gave it new powers. Congress could now force individual citizens to obey its laws, and if they disobeyed, the national (federal) courts dealt directly with them. Until now Congress could put pressure on an individual only through his State.

Under the Articles of Confederation the President's duties were almost limited to welcoming guests and giving them dinner. Now under the Constitution, the President of the United States became a combination of king and prime minister, one of the most powerful men of the world.

The Constitution defined his duties and qualifications and wrote his oath of office. It made him Commander in Chief of the armed forces, gave him the right to grant pardons and *reprieves*, make treaties 'with the advice and consent' of the Senate, appoint ambassadors and other officials such as Supreme Court Justices, call and *adjourn* Congress. He was to be elected for a term of four years, and could only be removed by *impeachment*. As John Adams said: 'The royal office in Poland is a mere shadow in comparison with it.' The Constitution also arranged for the election of the President, Vice President, Senators and Congressmen, and the appoint-
28   ment of judges and other officials.

Once the deadlocks were broken, matters moved fast. By now many delegates were tired and bored and wanted to go home. So many left that when the end came, only thirty-nine delegates were still in Philadelphia to vote.

On Monday afternoon, 10 September, a mass of notes was handed to a committee of five men headed by the debonair Pennsylvania lawyer, Gouverneur Morris. As Thomas Jefferson wrote the Declaration of Independence, so Morris wrote the Constitution of the United States. Morris and his committee worked so swiftly that the Constitution was printed and ready for voting by Wednesday. The whole aim of the document was 'of the greatest interest to every American—namely, the creation of a nation'.

Nobody there thought the new Constitution was perfect. Many had real doubts about it. But as Washington, who had sat all day and every day at the little table at the end of the long, stuffy room, while it was hotly debated, wrote to his friend the Marquis de Lafayette, in France: 'It seems to me a little short of a miracle that delegates of so many States, different in their manners, circumstances and prejudices, should unite in forming a system of national government.'

The Constitution was far too democratic for Alexander Hamilton, for example. In fact, disgusted at the way things were going, he had left Philadelphia in the middle of the Convention. However, he returned to sign it. He was the only signer from conservative New York State. The delegates were determined, despite their many disagreements, to present a united front to the country. There was at least one man from every State to walk up, in order of the States from North to South, to put his name to the Constitution.

When his turn came, frail old Franklin had to be carried to the voting desk. He then asked James Wilson to read aloud a letter he had written. This is what Franklin said in his letter:

'I confess that there are several parts of this Constitution which I do not at present approve, but I am not sure that I shall never approve them. . . . I agree to this Constitution with all its faults, if they are such, because I think a

29

General Government necessary for us. . . . I doubt too
whether any other Convention we can obtain may be able
to make a better Constitution.'

Madison wrote in his journal:

'Whilst the last members were signing, Doctor Franklin,
looking towards the President's Chair at the back of which
a rising sun happened to be painted, said that through the
three months he had often looked at the sun and wondered
whether it was meant to be rising or setting. "Now at
length", the old gentleman said, "I have the happiness
to know it is a rising, not a setting sun." '

7 We, the People

When Gouverneur Morris wrote the Constitution he began by giving the reasons for it. He stated them thus:

'We, the People of the United States, in order to form a more perfect Union, establish Justice, ensure Domestic *Tranquility*, provide for the common Defence, promote the general Welfare, and secure the Blessings of Liberty to ourselves and our Posterity, do ordain and establish this CONSTITUTION for the United States of America.'

But despite this imposing explanation, it was not easy to convince all thirteen States that this new Constitution was a necessary or desirable thing. It took nine months of struggle to get the new Constitution accepted by even nine States—the minimum number required to make it law. Unlike Washington, many people preferred the old, loose arrangement under the Articles of Confederation which had left the separate States so free.

First, they felt, and with reason, that under the Confederation their country had accomplished much since 1776. It had fought and won an eight-years war, and negotiated a favourable peace treaty. Secondly, there had been great gains in democracy. State governors were chosen by the people, not the king. The upper chambers of the State Legislatures were elected, not appointed. In some States men no longer had to own property before they could vote. The great estates of the exiled Tories had been divided up among their former tenants and other farmers. (The property of Sir John Johnson in New York State, after he fled to Canada, was divided into 10,000 small farms.) Wherever the Church of England had been the state Church, it was disestablished and no longer supported by taxes.

Third, under the Confederation a problem that could have been fatal to easy expansion across the American continent was solved. What was to happen to Americans who left their homes in the thirteen original States and moved into the new land in the West? Would they be considered colonials like their ancestors who had left England for America? Or could they carry their nation with them? A law, inspired by Thomas Jefferson just before he left on his diplomatic mission to France in 1784, had given the solution. The law said that when Americans settled in lands west of the mountains, the lands would first become Territories. When enough settlers had arrived, the Territories could be split up into States. These new States would become States of the United States, completely equal in every way with the original thirteen. The law also forbade slavery in these new States.

Fourth, their country had grown fast under the Confederation. Schools and colleges had opened. There were new towns, new markets, new artists, new writers. The American of the 1780s was a hopeful, boastful, self-reliant man. Why should he allow his government, that had done so much, to be destroyed in a secret meeting in Philadelphia?

Many of the farmers and frontiersmen also feared that the new government might become too strong and take back the liberty and equality they had fought to win. One old Massachusetts farmer said: 'They will get all the power and money in their own hands and swallow up us little folks.'

And there were things about the Constitutional Convention and Constitution itself that some Americans distrusted. Had not the delegates exceeded their authority when they did away with the Articles of Confederation and made an entirely new kind of government? Had not the Convention supposedly been called just to 'revise', and not destroy, the Articles of Confederation? Why, they asked, were the meetings all in secret? What went on all those months inside Independence Hall, that the rest of America should not know

James Madison, was one of the authors of 'The Federalist Papers', and the fourth President of the United States

about? Jefferson particularly, said that this secrecy was an 'abominable *precedent*'.

Since King George's taxes had been a big cause of the Revolution, why was Congress now given the power to tax? Suppose a President used the great power the Constitution gave him to make himself king?

One of the most frequent, serious and sound criticisms of the Constitution was the lack of the Bill of Rights—particularly 33 since most of the State Constitutions contained a Bill of Rights. What about trial by jury? '*Habeas corpus*'? Freedom of speech, religion, press and assembly? Why had none of these ancient British safeguards been written into the Constitution?

But the men who quit Independence Hall in September were determined that their country should have a strong, capable central government. In speeches before their State Legislatures, in pamphlets and articles they argued and pleaded for the Constitution.

Three of the ablest, Alexander Hamilton, James Madison and John Jay, began in October 1787, to publish a series of eighty-five articles explaining and defending the new Constitution. These articles, called 'The Federalist Papers', were written to persuade the people of New York State, whose governor, George Clinton, was the Constitution's great foe. 'The Federalist Papers' argued that a strong, national government was vital and the new government would have the 'checks and balances' needed to keep it from becoming a tyranny. James Madison pointed out: 'You must first enable the government to control the governed, and in the next place oblige it to control itself.'

Though they are by no means easy reading, 'The Federalist Papers' soon became best-sellers. They went into edition after edition, were debated in taverns as well as courts and council rooms. In trying to persuade the New Yorkers, Hamilton, Jay and Madison persuaded their whole country.

Just as important to ratification as 'The Federalist Papers' was a solemn promise: the first thing Congress would do in its first session would be to add a Bill of Rights to the Constitution.

There are almost as many opinions as there are historians on why one State accepted the Constitution, and another had to be bullied into it. (Hamilton bullied New York State into ratification by threatening that New York City would secede from the rest of the State if she didn't.) One explanation is that States like Delaware and Georgia, who were doing badly under the Articles, quickly ratified. The more prosperous States, such as Pennsylvania or Massachusetts, but which

REDEUNT SATURNIA REGNA.

On the erection of the Eleventh PILLAR of the great National DOME, we beg leave most sincerely to felicitate " OUR DEAR COUNTRY."

Rise it will.

☞ *The foundation good—it may yet be SAVED.*

The FEDERAL EDIFICE.
ELEVEN STARS, in quick succession rise—
ELEVEN COLUMNS strike our wond'ring eyes,
Soon o'er the *whole*, shall swell the beauteous DOME,
COLUMBIA's boast—and FREEDOM's hallow'd home.
  Here shall the ARTS in glorious splendour shine !
And AGRICULTURE give her stores divine !
COMMERCE refin'd, dispense us more than gold,
And this new world, teach WISDOM to the old—
RELIGION here shall fix her blest abode,
Array'd in *mildness*, like its parent GOD !
JUSTICE and LAW, shall endless PEACE maintain,
And *the* " SATURNIAN AGE," *return again.*

An American cartoon celebrating the ratification by 11 States—all but North Carolina and Rhode Island

still had some problems, needed persuasion, but accepted the Constitution quite soon. Rhode Island, New York, North Carolina and Virginia were the slowest to ratify. In Virginia the fight was fierce. Patrick Henry, the former governor and a great and patriotic leader since long before the Revolution, led the opposition. He had had real suspicions of the Convention's intentions from its beginning. 'Sir,' he said, 'I smelt a rat.' Rhode Island, although it was the smallest State of the thirteen, refused to ratify the Constitution until 1790, and meanwhile was outside of the United States.

This fierce struggle over ratification divided the country into two political parties: the Federalists were for the Constitution; the Anti-Federalists (or, as they came to be known, 35 the Republicans) opposed it. So this struggle started the two-party system, which has lasted in America ever since, though the men who wrote the Constitution neither expected nor wished it.

On 21 June, when New Hampshire voted 'yes', the Constitution had the approval of the nine States necessary for ratification. (Neither North Carolina nor Rhode Island had yet ratified, when Washington was inaugurated in April 1789.) The work of 'The Federalist Papers' was done. The delegates had pleaded and argued all through their home States to good effect. But the main reason why the American Constitution was accepted by most Americans was that Benjamin Franklin and George Washington accepted it. Their countrymen trusted them, their judgment and honesty.

Notice that the word 'constitution' means something quite different in Great Britain and in the United States. The British Constitution is an accumulation of customs and traditions gradually developing and changing over many centuries. It can be changed by Parliament in its ordinary, law-making processes. The American Constitution, on the other hand, is one document, written in one place, Philadelphia, Pennsylvania; during one summer, 1787. It can be changed only by a special legal process. Its changes are called 'amendments'. Well-known amendments are the 'Bill of Rights'; the amendment banning slavery in 1865; the amendment giving women the right to vote in 1920.

Everyone took it for granted that George Washington would be elected the first President of the young Republic. To his dismay, he was.

8 First in Peace

Thirteen sea captains dressed in blue and white rowed a 50-foot barge across New York Harbour. A *sloop* full of girls singing a new song 'God Save Great Washington' to an old tune, 'God Save the King' followed. A British man o' war boomed thirteen times as the barge passed. A Spanish ship broke out the flags of twenty nations.

The red-hung barge nosed up to a red-carpeted wharf. Cannon roared and church bells pealed as George Washington in his blue-and-buff soldier's uniform stepped on shore. After a seven-day triumphal journey from Mount Vernon he had arrived in New York City to be sworn in as President of the United States.

Late that night, feasts, fireworks and toasts to 'The Saviour of His Country' over, Washington wrote in his diary: 'I greatly fear my countrymen will expect too much from me.' As head of a new Republic, testing a new kind of government, he walked an 'untrodden path' and feared where it might lead.

New York City was the new capital of the new nation and wanted to remain so. She had built a handsome new Federal Hall for Congress and had torn down old Fort George, on the Harbour, to make room for a President's Mansion.

Seven days later, on 30 April 1789, on the balcony of Federal Hall, framed by red hangings and cheered by crowds below, George Washington was sworn in as President. He wore a dark brown suit of American cloth with eagles carved on the buttons and a dress sword in a plain steel scabbard. Close by, also in homespun, but as short and stout as Washington was

Left: *Federal Hall—Washington's inauguration.* Right: *The stars and stripes of Washington's coat of arms appear on the American flag also*

tall and stately, stood the new Vice President, John Adams of Massachusetts. It was Adams, who, back in 1775, had chosen Washington to head the American army. For many years he had been a diplomat in England, France and Holland.

Washington's hands quaked as he read his short speech. He later told his friend, Henry Knox, he had 'felt like a culprit going to his place of execution'.

Because money troubles had come near to wrecking the Articles of Confederation, money matters were Washington's first concern. He put his wartime secretary in charge of the country's shaky finances. Alexander Hamilton was only thirty-two when he became Secretary of the Treasury (similar to the Chancellor of the Exchequer). He is the youngest man ever to serve in a President's Cabinet.

Washington also worried about *etiquette*, or what he called 'deportment'. What was he to be called? Adams, fresh from royal European courts wanted 'state and pomp'. He argued that Washington's title should be 'His Highness President of the United States and Protector of the Rights of the Same'; and that Washington should be addressed, 'Your Mightiness'. Squabbles over Washington's title delayed his inauguration three days. When Congress finally decreed he should be called, simply 'Mr President', Washington wrote: 'Happily the matter is now done, I hope never to be revived.'

Washington soon saw that if he kept up the cordial around-the-clock hospitality of Mount Vernon he would 'be unable to attend to any business whatsoever'. To save time and strength he limited his entertaining strictly to two functions a week: a stiff evening *levee*, and a livelier drawing room where Mrs Washington received.

The Washingtons' first home in New York City was on Cherry Street, where the Brooklyn Bridge now begins. The house was too small. Three of the President's secretaries shared an attic room. One, the poet David Humphreys, kept the other two awake while he paced the floor in his night-shirt reciting verses. After a year the Washingtons moved to the beautiful McComb Mansion on Bowling Green near the

Harbour. It stood on a wide, fashionable street. A dozen different languages drifted through the windows. Even then New York was cosmopolitan.

New York City in the 1790s was a bustling, business city of English and Dutch-style houses. Thirty thousand people lived near the water's edge, one-ninth were Negroes; two-thirds of the Negroes, slaves. There was no sewage system. Pigs ran wild in the street eating refuse. This, of course, meant many epidemics. There were no water pipes. Fires were put out by volunteer firemen, each man bringing his own leather water bag. There were so many bad fires in early New York City that few of the original buildings still stand.

Washington rode about in a big canary-coloured coach carved with nymphs and cupids, the stars and stripes of his family coat of arms painted on the door. A true Virginian, he loved horses. Six magnificent white ones, with hooves polished coal black, drew his gold coach. Washington's wife, Martha— or as stylish New Yorkers called her, Lady Washington—was a plump, gracious woman who found her restricted life dull. 'I think I am more like a state prisoner than anything else', she said. But she was tactful, discreet and flawlessly kind—a popular and model First Lady for the young Republic.

Beside Hamilton, Washington chose two more old friends to help start his government. One was 300-pound Henry Knox, the former Chief of Artillery. It was Knox who back in 1776 dragged the great guns of Ticonderoga down to Boston and forced the British to give up the city. Washington named Knox Secretary of War. Washington wanted Thomas Jefferson, the author of the Declaration of Independence, to be his Secretary of State (Foreign Secretary). For the past six years Jefferson had been a diplomat in France. He was now on the high seas sailing home, with no idea of what Washington planned for him.

For months before Washington came, Hamilton had been living in New York. He and James Madison, now a Congressman from Virginia, had been hard at work making plans for the new government.

Since 1792 stocks and bonds have been sold on Wall Street in New York City. Brokers met under a buttonwood tree

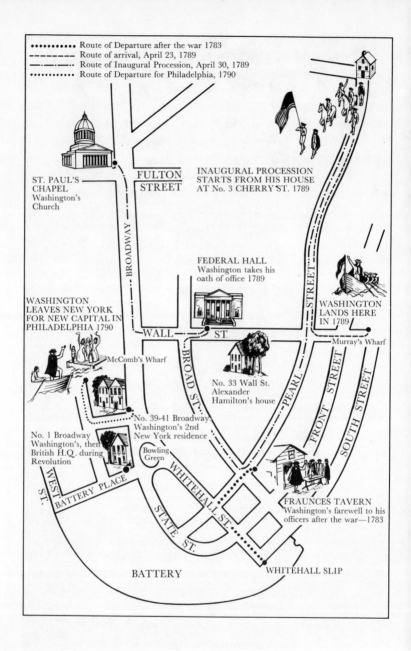

Map 4–*A map of George Washington's New York City*

Years later people still remembered how the two short, slim young men strode New York's cobbled streets in eager talk; how they stopped to play with a monkey tethered in a neighbour's yard. Madison was bright-eyed, frail, dressed in black; Hamilton, erect and elegant, his smile dazzling. Together Hamilton and Madison had written 'The Federalist Papers', together they had fought to get the Constitution ratified. Now they were determined it should work.

Hamilton's first aim as Secretary of the Treasury was to restore his penniless country's credit. Ten days after he took office, Congress asked his advice on how to do this. In January 1790 his 'Report on Public Credit' urged Congress to pay not only the national debts, at home and abroad, but to pay the States' debts too. The combined debts came to over 80 million dollars—a huge sum on which Congress didn't even have enough money to pay interest.

Most people agreed that the national government should try to pay what it owed—the 'price of liberty'. But there was a fight at once about the States' debts. States that had suffered great losses during the eight years' Revolution welcomed Hamilton's plan. Edanus Burke of South Carolina said his State could no more 'grapple with her enormous debt than a boy of twelve years of age is able to grapple with a giant'. But States who were well off opposed the proposal. New Hampshire said, 'If they have involved themselves in debt, it is their misfortune.'

After much argument, in April 1790, Hamilton's Assumption Bill (to pay all the debts) came to a vote in Congress. It was defeated by thirty-one to twenty-nine. Senator William Maclay of Pennsylvania, one of the Bill's (and Washington's) sharpest critics, mocked its disappointed supporters. One, he said, acted like a turkey or a goose nearly strangled. Another's mouth curved down like a horseshoe and the third hid his grief under the rim of a round hat.

But Alexander Hamilton, who had bullied New York State into accepting the Constitution, did not give up easily. He sought for a plan to get the big State of Virginia to vote for 43 his bill. By now Thomas Jefferson, the Virginian, was Secretary of State and in New York City, too. One day Hamilton and Jefferson met on Washington's door step. Hamilton looked 'haggard, sombre and dejected'. Back and forth he walked Jefferson, lamenting that if the Assumption Bill didn't become a law, 'our credit will burst and the States separate everyone to take care of itself'.

Jefferson listened. He invited Hamilton, Madison and two other Virginia congressmen to dinner. The men talked long by candlelight. Hamilton knew that Virginia wanted to get the nation's capital moved southwards. So finally he and Jefferson got Madison to promise that Virginia would vote for Assumption, if in return Hamilton's New Yorkers would vote to move the nation's capital down south to Virginia. It was a deal!

So on 10 July 1790 the Residence Act, which moved the nation's capital down south to Virginia, became law. Philadelphia, in Pennsylvania, was to be the capital for the next ten years. (This gave time to build a new Federal City on the banks of the Potomac River in Virginia.) In 1800, when the ten years were up, this new Federal City (Washington) would become the national capital. Three weeks later Congress voted again on the Assumption Bill. This time it passed.

When the tale of the Jefferson-Hamilton deal leaked out, the foes of Assumption were disgusted. 'We may as well have a set of gamblers for rulers', they muttered. Jefferson distrusted businessmen. He was happy to have the national capital far away from a big city like New York or Philadelphia, dominated by rich merchants. Hamilton rejoiced that his country's credit could become strong at last.

But the year-long quarrel over Assumption, following so soon after the fight over ratification of the Constitution, showed that already in America there was a deep division on how the country should be run.

9 Duel of Giants

When George Washington chose Hamilton and Jefferson to help him run his government, he believed they were the best men for the jobs and would '*harmonize* extremely well together'. Before his first term was up, he saw how right he was on the first point, how wrong on the second.

Hamilton believed that since everything the government did involved money, he as Secretary of the Treasury, had a right to meddle in any foreign, domestic or military concerns he wanted to. He felt his job was the same as the British Prime Minister's. (For this Jefferson mocked him as a 'servile copyist of Mr Pitt'.) Also, although Jefferson was appointed Secretary of State in September, he did not come to New York to take over his duties until the following March. This gave Hamilton time to get a firm grip on the government, especially its foreign affairs.

Hamilton felt British friendship and trade were vital to American safety and prosperity; that a strong central government and sound credit were essential. He wanted American businessmen to play a big role in governing the country.

Hamilton was born in the West Indies and came to America when he was sixteen. Therefore, unlike most Americans of his day, his first loyalty was to the national government, not his home State. Next to George Washington, Hamilton was the most 'nation-minded' man in the country. He had settled in New York City and married one of its heiresses, Betsy, General Philip Schuyler's daughter. Time passed. Now in his thirties, his rebel days were behind him, and Hamilton became daily more conservative and pro-British.

The long-legged, red-headed aristocrat, Thomas Jefferson, was his complete opposite. He was a Virginia landowner, master of 10,000 acres. A good lawyer, he had no head for business and considered farmers the 'chosen people of God'. (America, he once wrote, was the only country where farmers read Homer.) Although he was a weak public speaker, he was a brilliant writer, read eight languages, was a subtle diplomat, and grew to be a master politician. Before he became Secretary of State he had spent six years in Europe, close to the tyrannical, frivolous French court and the then corrupt British one. He saw Europe as a world of cruel injustices where 'every man was either a hammer or an anvil'.

When Jefferson finally arrived in New York City in March 1790, he was shocked to see a growing 'preference of kingly over republican government' and angry at the way Hamilton interfered with foreign policy. Hamilton was a close friend of a British secret agent, Major George Beckwith. He told Beckwith many state secrets, particularly what went on in Cabinet meetings. The British Foreign Office code name for Hamilton was No. 7.

In the eleven months since Washington's inauguration much had been done. The promised Bill of Rights had been passed. A Supreme Court, three circuit courts, and thirteen district courts had been set up. 'With singular pleasure' George Washington had invited John Jay, the New York lawyer and co-author of 'The Federalist Papers' to be the the first Chief Justice of the Supreme Court.

Congress was also raising money to pay the national debts. It was selling land in the West. It was taxing imports and both foreign and home-made whisky. Jefferson called the tax on American-made whisky 'odious'. He felt it was unfair to farmers. Whisky was made from grain. It was the farmers' chief source of cash, because a whole year's crop of grain, distilled into whisky, could be carried to market in kegs on one mule's back.

As we saw in the last chapter, Madison, Jefferson and Hamilton had worked together at first, co-operating on the   47

Assumption and Residence Acts. But when Hamilton wanted to start a national bank (like the Bank of England) and a Mint to make money Jefferson and Madison objected. They accused him of overstepping the power the Constitution gave him. They also felt he favoured business interests over the farmers, who after all made up 90 per cent of the population.

Although Washington was a Virginia landowner like Jefferson, he was closer in politics to Hamilton. Like Hamilton he could not forget how his Army had suffered during the Revolution because the government had been too poor and weak to pay them. Like Hamilton he believed in as strong a government as 'was consistent with liberty'. He was never Hamilton's pawn (as some people said), but he backed more and more of Hamilton's ideas. And because Washington backed them, the Bank of the United States was founded in 1791 and the United States Mint in 1792.

As Jefferson saw Hamilton getting his way, he became more worried. He began to imagine that Hamilton wanted to change the American Republic into a kingdom. Although a few years before Jefferson had said, 'If I could not go to Heaven but with a party, I would not go there at all', he set out now to build a political party that would be strong enough to defeat Hamilton and his plans.

Many other Americans, like Jefferson, worried about what Hamilton was up to, and resented the way Washington backed him. Senator Maclay said, 'Mr Hamilton is all-powerful and fails in nothing he attempts', and added 'the President has become in the hands of Hamilton the dirty dish clout over every speculation, as his name goes to wipe away blame.'

So Jefferson and Madison, early in the summer of 1791, set out on what they called a 'botanizing expedition' all through New York State. For a month they visited and talked politics with every leading anti-Hamilton politician they could — Governor George Clinton; Aaron Burr (the head of Tammany Hall, the New York City political machine), Chancellor Robert Livingston. They also visited Revolutionary battle-fields, and, as Jefferson wrote to his daughter, enjoyed the wild strawberries and trout fishing.

As members of the President's Cabinet, Hamilton and Jefferson could not attack each other openly. So each one found a newspaper editor to do it for him. In April 1789 Hamilton arranged for John Fenno to start the 'Gazette of the United States'. In October 1791 Jefferson persuaded Madison's Princeton College classmate, the poet, Philip Freneau, to edit an opposition paper, the 'National Gazette'. Now Jefferson and Hamilton each had a mouthpiece to call the other names, and attack his plans.

It is important to remember that both Hamilton and Jefferson were brilliant men and good patriots, anxious to serve and strengthen their country. But each man's dream for

Philadelphia was the capitol of the United States in the 1790s

America was completely different, and in his opponent's eyes, dangerous. In fact Hamilton and Jefferson are as important in American history as political symbols, as for what they accomplished. Each stands for a conflicting political movement. Hamilton represents the believer in a strong, centralised government; Jefferson in increasing equality and freedom. After 200 years, politicians in either camp still quote and misquote both of them for their own political ends.

Hamilton believed in a balanced and varied economy. Jefferson wanted a farming society. Hamilton believed in strong government. Jefferson maintained that he was 'not a friend to a very energetic government' (although when he became President his way of governing was at times very energetic). Hamilton felt that the upper classes should rule. Jefferson was sure that ordinary people, if educated, could govern themselves well.

As George Washington's first term as President came near its end in 1792 he wanted very much to retire and go home to farming and Mount Vernon. But Hamilton and Jefferson, despite their disputes, agreed on one thing. The country, as Jefferson said, was not yet strong enough 'to try to walk alone'. They urged Washington to stay in office. They warned him that the thirteen States might drift apart if he didn't. 'North and South will hang together, if they have you to hang on', Jefferson told Washington.

Reluctantly Washington accepted another four-year term as President, but he begged his two Secretaries to become friends again. To Jefferson he lamented the internal *dissensions* 'harrowing and tearing our *vitals*'. He urged Hamilton to 'have charity in deciding on the opinions and actions of others'. It was no use. As Jefferson wrote years later, he and Alexander Hamilton were 'daily pitted in the cabinet like fighting cocks'.

10 Indians! Indians!

Secretary of War Henry Knox faced hard problems too. Toughest of all were the Indians on the northwest frontier. 'To awe the Indians' was Washington's chief reason for asking Congress to build up the army, and also to 'protect our Trade, prevent the *encroachment* of our Neighbours of Canada and the Floridas and guard us, at least, from surprise'.

In the Peace Treaty that ended the Revolution, Great Britain promised to give up five forts that were also important fur-trading posts. They stood on the St Lawrence River and the banks of the Great Lakes, below the American side of the Canadian-American border. But Canadian settlers and fur traders objected so much that the British government secretly told the Governor of Canada, Lord Dorchester, not to hand over the forts to the United States. The Americans had been very slow in paying what they owed the Loyalists and British merchants under the same treaty. England made this slowness her excuse for keeping the five strategic forts.

The early Republic never wanted a standing army. Back in 1776 Sam Adams had told General Horatio Gates: 'We don't choose to trust you generals with too much power for too long at a time.' Also during the Revolution, and long after, Americans cherished the wrong and costly belief that volunteer militia would do instead of a trained army, that an American farmer with a gun could beat any foreign soldier.

So in 1783 the unpaid American Army was sent home. By 1789 there were less than 800 officers and men scattered among the frontier forts. Their main action was against American settlers pushing into Indian land.

Left: *Chief Little Turtle*
Below: *A frontier fort*

By now the Indians realised that the American government couldn't or wouldn't curb the land-grabbing settlers. So, as we saw, Indian raids became so frequent and ferocious that some settlers threatened to appeal for aid to the Spanish beyond the Mississippi River or to the English army in Canada. This threat made General Knox and Washington act.

Two old soldiers were put in charge of the Northwest frontier, hard-drinking Josiah Harmar and gouty Arthur St Clair.

Harmar led the first campaign against the Indians. In September 1791 he set out with a ramshackle troop of 1,453 (of which only 320 were Regular Army). After a seventeen-day march he reached the main village of the Miami Indians, near present day Fort Wayne, Indiana. The Indians didn't wait for the American attack. They set fire to their village and hid in the woods. Harmar sent Colonel John Hardin six miles down a forest trail. Suddenly warwhoops came from all sides, yells and gunfire. It was an ambush by Chief Little Turtle and 700 braves. The militia panicked and scattered. Of the regular soldiers only two survived: an ensign stumbled behind a log and stayed hidden; a captain neck-deep in a swamp, watched all night while his comrades were tortured and killed.

The Indians were elated by their victory, their first since General Sullivan had beaten them at Newtown, N.Y., during the Revolution. One hundred Americans were slain, only twenty Indians. Indian attacks on frontier families grew fiercer.

St. Clair led the next campaign. Before St Clair left for his post in the West, George Washington, an old Indian fighter himself, had warned, 'Again and again, General, beware of surprise.'

St Clair was ordered to build a string of forts. He had built three by 3 November, and marched his army about 100 miles north of Cincinnati, Ohio, camping near the headwaters of the Wabash River. There were signs of Indians lurking near.   53

During the night sentries heard turkey calls—ancient Indian war signals. They didn't warn their officers. Next morning while the soldiers were cooking breakfast 'the Indians came on with the warwhoop . . . in a few minutes all round our army—behind every tree, stump and log with their rifles they cut down our men'. Again the untrained militia panicked. Old St Clair had three horses shot from under him and lost half his army. More than 800 were wounded or killed.

Weeks passed before the news crossed the snowy mountains and ice-filled rivers to George Washington. He was giving a dinner party when it came, and said nothing. After his guests were gone he stormed up and down, saying, again and again that he warned St Clair against just such a surprise attack.

By now the Indians were sure the settlers could be driven away. Their raids intensified. The terrified settlers begged the American government to sue for peace. So again the government changed its Indian policy. It blamed the settlers for being too violent. Jefferson advised: 'We must do as the

Map 5–War with Indians on the Old Northwest frontier; towns and battlefields are marked

Spaniards and English do, keep the Indians in peace by liberal and constant presents.' So messengers to the Indians were told to try to persuade them that the Americans did not want to take their lands away.

In 1790, the western Indians met in a great council. The Iroquois (a powerful eastern tribe) sent delegates who urged their western kinsmen to come to terms with the Americans. However, the British encouraged the western tribes to hold out—being very careful, the while, not to promise to go to war against America on the Indians' behalf. The western tribes listened to the British. After twenty-four months of negotiation, they said to the Americans: If you want peace, the settlers must go back across the Ohio River, and the Ohio River must be made 'a permanent boundary between your land and ours'.

When the Americans made an offer to buy the Indians' land 'for such a large sum of money or goods as never before has been given since white people put foot on this inland', the Indians answered:

'Brothers: We know the settlers are poor or they would never have crossed the Ohio River. Give them the money instead and also sums it will cost to raise armies.

'Brothers: You have talked to us about concessions. It appears strange that you expect any from us. We have only been defending our just rights against your invasion. We want peace. Restore to us our country and we shall be enemies no longer.'

But the American government did not plan, then or ever, to give the Indians' *ancestral* lands back to them.

11 Fear of France

The French Revolution 'drew a red-hot ploughshare' through the history of America as well as France. It inflamed the conflicts between the Federalists and Republicans, the east and the western frontier, between Hamilton and Jefferson.

At first most Americans rejoiced when their old friends, the French, had a revolution of their own. They celebrated with balls and dinner parties, called each other Citizen and Citizeness, and sang the Ça Ira. 'Liberty has another feather in her cap', they cried and cheered when Lafayette sent the key to the main gate of the Bastille prison to Washington. Lafayette wrote that it was a gift 'from the missionary of liberty to its patriarch'. (The key is still displayed at Mount Vernon.)

But Washington worried. He foresaw 'rocks and shoals not visible at present' that could wreck the French government.

It took a long time for news to cross the Atlantic. In November 1792 the Americans heard that France had declared 'a war of all people against all kings' and was fighting Austria and Prussia. A winter of fierce storms followed. Not until April did more news come—news that horrified Washington, Adams and many other Federalists. King Louis XVI's head had been chopped off. France was also at war with England, Spain and Holland.

All over America the 'smouldering coal pit of faction' blazed up. Federalist ladies wore black roses to mourn the French king. Republicans said his death was 'just the execution of another malefactor'. Washington's cabinet was

split. Though neither man wanted America to go to war,

Jefferson sided with France, Hamilton with England. Washington, knowing the United States was too 'young and weak a Republic' to survive war, gladly took Hamilton's view that the French-American treaty was no longer binding. It had been made with King Louis. The French Republic had murdered King Louis.

So, though for Jefferson's sake, he left the word *neutrality* out of his proclamation, Washington on 22 April 1793 announced that America would 'pursue a conduct friendly and impartial' to all countries at war. He also forbade Americans to help either side.

Keeping America neutral was hard, because the newly arrived French envoy, Edmond Charles Genet (known in American history as Citizen Genet) was doing his best to drag America into the war on the French side. His orders were to get all the help he could for France from George Washington, to fit out American ships to attack the British, to recruit an American army to fight for France against the Spanish in the West and the English to the North.

Genet made such trouble that soon even the pro-French Jefferson was urging he be sent home. Jefferson wrote that Genet was 'hot-headed, all imagination, no judgment, passionate, disrespectful and even indecent towards the President'; that 'he would sink the Republican interests if they do not abandon him'. But Washington, fearing that Genet would be guillotined if he were shipped home to France, let him stay on as a private citizen. Genet married New York Governor Clinton's daughter and became a gentleman farmer on the Hudson River.

Nowhere in America was the French Revolution welcomed as warmly as on the western frontier. Jefferson's Republican Clubs renamed themselves Jacobin Clubs. (The Federalists called them '*demoniacal* clubs.') Discontented frontier leaders accepted commissions in the 'French Legion on the Mississippi River' and began enlisting men to fight against the Spanish in Florida and to the west. This really scared the American government. Spain and England had signed an alliance 57 against France. If the frontier 'legionnaires' attacked the Spanish, America could be dragged into war with both Spain and England.

So, to conciliate the settlers, embittered by Indian attacks, the American government again switched its Indian policy from peace-making to war. But this time Washington and Knox sent out no hard-drinking Harmar or gouty St Clair, but a hero of the Revolutionary war, famous for his daring, Mad Anthony Wayne.

In 1792 General Wayne led an army of 1,200 into the Northwest Territory. He wintered in Greenville, Ohio, building a string of forts and drilling, drilling his men. He kept so many sentries on alert the Indians called him a 'chief who never sleeps—he is like a black snake, the night and day are alike to him'.

When after months of training, his men still fled before a small Indian attack, Wayne made up his mind not to risk any more battles until he was sure of winning. Winter passed, Spring, and another Winter. Still Wayne waited and worked.

Finally after two years, in August 1794, Wayne decided it was time to fight. He marched 3,000 soldiers to the Indian headquarters near British-held Fort Miami near present-day Toledo, Ohio. Mad Anthony Wayne had strict orders from Washington. He was to avoid risking a war with England, unless there was no other way to beat the Indians. In that case he would have to take the chance.

Wayne sent a final message to the Indian chiefs saying the British neither could nor would fight for the Indians. Little Turtle hid his braves behind a two-mile wide belt of great trees which storms had uprooted and spread thick on the ground. (This is why the battle is called The Battle of Fallen Timbers.) Wayne delayed for three days. The Indians who always fasted on the eve of a fight, waited too, hourly growing hungrier and more jumpy.

At dawn, 20 August 1794, Wayne attacked. His men advanced in a bayonet charge against Indian musket fire. The Indian line broke. Sixteen hundred mounted Kentucky riflemen vaulted the thickness of fallen tree trunks as though they rode a steeplechase. The Indians fled back toward the British fort. Had the fort gates opened for the Indians, with the Americans pressing close behind, war between England and America could have begun. But the British didn't open the fort gates. The Indians ran on, cursing them, into the woods.

For three days Wayne camped near Fort Miami. If either side had fired a shot, war could have started, as unintentionally, as years before it had at Lexington. But this time, the men on both sides were disciplined soldiers. No shot was fired. Ruthlessly Wayne burnt miles of Indian homes and grainfields golden for harvest. The British commandant protested but did nothing to stop him. Mission completed, Wayne marched back to Cincinnati, Ohio.

While Wayne prepared for battle with the Indians, Washington worked for understanding with the warring countries across the Atlantic. There was serious trouble now with England over sea trade as well as frontier forts and national boundaries.

When in 1793 France went to war with England, Holland and Spain, America welcomed this chance to make money by trading with both sides. Jefferson said: 'I hope France, England and Spain will see it to their interest to let us make bread for them in peace and to give us a good price for it.'

France, of course, didn't want America to supply her foe, England; nor England, her foe, France. England had a strong navy to thwart America. She clamped on a blockade, seizing 300 American ships in the first year of the war. British men o' war halted and searched American ships carrying goods to French ports. And if, during the search, they found any British sailors in the American crew, they arrested them and took them off. This was a custom in the British Navy toward British merchant ships. If a British warship lost men in battle, she would halt the next British merchantman she met, and take off as many sailors as she needed to fill out her crew. Americans called this behaviour 'impressing sailors'. It made them furious.

59

At this time there were a good many British deserters on American ships, where they were better paid, fed and treated, and didn't have to fight. Some of the deserters had become American citizens—not that this protected them. The British didn't recognise their right to do so. Also, if a British naval captain needed crewmen he didn't always check too carefully to see if an able-bodied young man was English-born or not, and took an occasional American, too.

So as the war dragged on, more American ships were halted, more American crewmen impressed, and there was more American resentment. Washington saw ill-feeling growing to war point. To try 'to prevent war, if justice can be done', in April 1794 he asked John Jay to give up his post on the Supreme Court, and go as Envoy Extraordinary to England to talk things over.

American historians still disagree about the treaty which John Jay, with the greatest difficulty, finally negotiated with England in November 1794. England agreed, at last, to return the five frontier forts and made concessions on East and West Indian trade. No mention was made in the treaty of impressing sailors or stopping American ships.

Both Jay and his treaty were savagely attacked in America. Jefferson called it 'the death warrant of American liberty'. Hamilton was stoned when he defended it. A mob hanged Jay in effigy, and one newspaper said his lips should have been 'blistered to the bone' because he kissed the Queen of England's hand. However, Washington believed it was the best treaty Jay could get in the circumstances, and backed it. Because Washington backed it, Congress in June 1795 ratified the Jay Treaty.

When Spain saw her ally, England, coming to terms with America, she felt she had better do the same. So in October 1795 in the Treaty of San Lorenzo the long Spanish-American dispute over the Florida border was settled. In this treaty Spain also gave American frontiersmen permission to ship their goods down the Mississippi River and use the Port of

New Orleans for the next three years.

Treaty of Greenville—peace with the Indians. (Courtesy Chicago Historical Society)

You can imagine how angry France became when America, whom she had helped to free, made these treaties with her two worst enemies. In revenge she captured and confiscated American ships, too. In 1796 and 1797, France seized 340 American ships.

If the French were enraged at the Jay Treaty, the Indians were heartsick. The news that the English were giving up the frontier forts that had supplied and supported them for years, filled them with despair. They had been forsaken by their old ally. So in the summer of 1795, 1,000 Indian chieftains representing twelve Indian nations met with representatives of the Fifteen Fires (the fifteen United States). In August they signed the Treaty of Greenville ceding the south, central and east of what is now the State of Ohio to the Americans. Like Napoleon across the sea, the Indians, having won all their other battles, lost their last, and their war—a thirteen-year war that killed more Americans than all the major battles of the American Revolution together.

By now Washington's second term as President was almost over. Both Hamilton and Jefferson had left him—Hamilton to practise law in New York City, Jefferson to farm Monticello; both to work secretly and constantly against each other's policies.

Washington had never wanted to be President. He had worked hard without salary for eight years to make America strong and keep her at peace. Foreign meddling had been stopped; boundary disputes with England and Spain settled; the Indian frontier calmed. She had an organised government, sound credit, courts, growing trade and education. The Federal government's authority over the States and right to tax them had been secured, and all the time the balance between liberty and order had been maintained. Despite the few and horrible roads, 'on horseback, dressed in his old continental uniform, with his hat off', Washington had toured most of the country, seeing and being seen by his fellow Americans.

After eight years of such toil, Washington was not only tired and homesick for Mount Vernon, but angry and hurt. Ever since he had proclaimed American neutrality in the French war, pro-French Republican newspapers had attacked him. Resentment over the Jay Treaty made the attacks worse. Washington was not only criticised for his foreign policies, now, but for his way of life. They said he was an ape of royalty who surrounded himself by mushroom lordlings and court *satellites*. He was called a '*supercilious* tyrant' and in his 'political *dotage*'. Washington, a very sensitive man, bore these slanders with painful patience until one day he saw a cartoon of himself crowned and kneeling by a guillotine. Then he cried out that 'he would rather be in his grave than President of United States, or on his farm than be made Emperor of the World'.

So, determined to retire, in September 1796, he sent for the editor of a small Philadelphia newspaper and gave him thirty-two handwritten sheets of paper to print. It was his famous 'Farewell Address'. Washington urged his countrymen to

A Mourning Memorial to Washington

value their union and liberty, to steer clear of permanent foreign alliances, to nurture education. He warned against too much party spirit and the danger that the country might break up geographically and split in two (as happened in the Civil War). It was, as he wrote 'the *disinterested* warning of a parting friend'.

In March 1797 John Adams, his Vice President, succeeded him. Adams reported to his wife how Washington looked on his last day as President 'Methought I heard him say, "Ay, I am fairly out, you are fairly in! See which one of us will be the happiest." '

Washington left the next day for Mount Vernon. He had written to Knox that he never wanted to go twenty miles 63 away from home again. Two peaceful years were left to him. Though he never interfered, his advice and backing were often sought.

In December 1799, at the age of sixty-seven, in the last month of the last year of the eighteenth century, George Washington died. He was mourned the world over. Flags flew at half mast in the British Channel Fleet. Napoleon draped his war trophies in black.

Now, 170 years later, British historians proudly claim George Washington as 'an exceptionally fine example of the old-fashioned English country gentleman'. At home he has had his critics, but to most Americans he has always been what his old friend Richard Henry Lee called him in final tribute: 'First in War, First in Peace, First in the hearts of his countrymen.'

12   Honest John Yankee

'I was John Yankee and such I shall live and die.'

John Adams followed Washington as President of the United States, beating Thomas Jefferson by seventy-one to sixty-eight votes. Adams was 'President by Three Votes' only. His foes never let him forget it. Jefferson became the new Vice President.

Adams, a learned, sixty-one-year-old New England lawyer, had a sharp mind and tongue. Despite his cranky ways both Washington and Jefferson appreciated him. Washington judged Adams a 'reasonable and honest person'. Jefferson said he was 'always an honest man, often a great one, but sometimes absolutely mad'.

Though Adams had given Washington his start when he made him General of the Army back in 1775, by 1797 he was not a little jealous of him. He muttered that Washington 'only got the reputation of being a great man because he kept his mouth shut'. Adams rarely could. Adams disliked being Vice President, 'the most insignificant office ever invention of man contrived'. His main job, presiding over the Senate, was a trial to him. It was punishment 'to hear men talk five hours a day and not be at liberty to talk at all'.

Conservative, Federalist Adams was accused by his enemies of being pro-British and a monarchist. This wasn't true; though he certainly preferred law-abiding England to Terrorist France. He 'didn't know what to make of a republic of thirty million atheists'. While a diplomat in England, Adams had grown to like George III. When they first met, Adams said he hoped 'the old good nature and the old good

65

John Adams—second President of the United States

humour' would return between their countries. King George
had answered that although he 'was the last to consent to the
separation' he was the first 'to meet the friendship of the
United States as an independent power'. Adams enjoyed
King George's conversation so much that at court he spoke
to him whenever he could, and eavesdropped when he could
not!

Although he liked the King, Adams was as determined as
Washington to keep America out of England's war with
France. He felt that America had been 'a football between
contending nations' too long. He didn't mean it to happen
while he was President. He believed that 'free ships meant
free trade' and that Americans had a right to sell their goods
to both France and England. The countries at war disagreed

and continued to blockade and capture American ships.

The French were still angry about the Jay Treaty when Adams took office. But Adams had 'it much at heart to settle all disputes with France' and sent a special envoy to Paris. The French threatened to arrest his envoy. Now war with France seemed near. In May 1797 Adams asked Congress for money to build up the Army and Navy. The pro-French Republicans called his speech a 'warwhoop'. When Adams imposed a Stamp Tax (memories of the Boston Tea Party!) the Republicans attacked the more.

But Adams kept trying for an understanding with France. His next three envoys were told they would have to pay a large bribe if they wanted the French to negotiate. This insult enraged the Federalists. They shouted 'Millions for defence, but not one cent for tribute', and set to work building and arming ships. For the next two years America and France fought an 'undeclared war' at sea. Many years later Adams wrote that America, during his presidency, was divided three ways. One-third was for England, one-third for France, one-third neutral.

Right from the start Adams made two bad mistakes. He kept Washington's Cabinet on, not realising that three out of the four men were Hamilton's tools, reporting back and taking orders from him. Hamilton scoffed at Adams as 'a mere old woman and unfit for President'. Adams also spent too much time away from the government in his handsome home in Quincy, Massachusetts, with its fine library, mahogany-panelled dining room, and imported furniture. While Washington was President he was at Mount Vernon only 181 days in eight years. During his four years in office Adams spent 385 days, or over one-quarter of the time, at home in Quincy, and his political enemies took good advantage of his absence.

Then, in 1800, John Adams and his wife Abigail, in accordance with the Residence Act, had to move with the nation's capital from Philadelphia, the 'finest town and best built' in America, to the new Federal City (now Washington, D.C.) 67 on the banks of the Potomac River in Virginia. The White House was barely begun. Only six of the thirty rooms had plaster on the walls. For two years there was no staircase between the first and second floor. The grounds were a mass of mudholes and rubbish. The Adamses spent more time than ever at Quincy.

Since the Reign of Terror started, French exiles had swarmed into America. A New Yorker bragged that he 'jostled ex-kings, and ex-empresses, and ex-nobles' every day on Broadway. The refugees made a living in town by teaching dancing, French, cooking and duelling. In the country they planted herb gardens and vineyards, made perfume and wine.

By the time Adams became President, the French had come to mean more than dancing lessons and wine-making to many Americans. They meant danger. France and America seemed on the edge of war—which side would these refugees take?

John Adams might declare, 'France shall do as she pleases and take her own course, America isn't scared.' This wasn't so. Congress was scared and in June and July of 1798 passed harsh laws against the French and other newcomers to America. These were the Alien and Sedition Acts. They extended the time needed to become an American citizen from five to fourteen years. They empowered the President to deport any 'dangerous aliens'. They set fines of up to $2,000, and jail terms up to two years for anyone convicted of speaking ill of a government official. Adams, a good lawyer, reluctantly signed the bills.

The Republicans raised a hullabaloo over the 'Federal Reign of Terror'. Thomas Jefferson (though because he was the Vice President he had to do it secretly) led the protests. He and Madison together wrote the Kentucky and Virginia Resolutions defying the Alien and Sedition Acts. These Resolutions claimed that since the Federal government had been created by the States, the States didn't owe it 'unlimited obedience'. These Resolutions were an early sign of the States Rights movements, which sixty years later flared up into Civil War.

Sea battle in the 'Undeclared War' between France and the United States

Time passed. The French did not declare war. Adams decided that 'there is no more prospect of seeing a French army here than there is in heaven'. Though his public statements were still 'warwhoops', he planned a new peace mission to Paris. An American diplomat in Holland had sent him secret word that the French, hard-pressed by Great Britain, would receive anybody America sent 'as an envoy of an independent and powerful nation'. So, one February day, while Congress debated a bill on 'encouraging the capture of French armed vessels', Adams astounded it with the news that he was going to send a new peace mission to France.

The Federalists were stunned by Adams's seeming about-face. Hamilton wrote a furious pamphlet calling him a liar, ingrate and unfit for office. Under Hamilton's attack the Federalist party split in two. This broke its hold on the government. In the 1800 election—a savage campaign of lies and name-calling—Jefferson's Republican party defeated the divided Federalists.

Jefferson became the third President of the United States. 69

He took office determined to calm and reunite his politics-torn country, and to put it back on the 'republican tack'. Adams, grim in defeat, left Washington before Jefferson's inauguration. His stand had cost him the Presidency but he felt proud and sure of one thing and he wanted it cut one day into his gravestone: 'Here lies John Adams who took upon himself the responsibility of the peace with France in the year 1800.'

However, it is not as a peacemaker that the old Yankee, John Adams, is best remembered, but as the founder of the Adams family. The Adams family with two Presidents (himself and his son, John Quincy) statesmen, scholars, diplomats, and writers has played a role in American history comparable to the Cecils and Churchills in England.

13   Jefferson in Triumph

Rejoice, Columbia's sons, rejoice,
To tyrants never bend the knee.
But join with heart and soul and voice
For Jefferson and Liberty.

It took six days of voting and thirty-six ballots to settle which
of the two leading Republicans would be next President—
Thomas Jefferson or the Tammany chieftain, charming,
spendthrift, Aaron Burr. Jefferson defeated Burr only because
he had Hamilton's backing. Hamilton considered Jefferson a
humbug, but Burr a scoundrel; so he put his tremendous
political power behind Jefferson. Jefferson became President
by two votes. Burr was the new Vice President.

In victory, Jefferson was a peacemaker. In his soothing
inaugural address he said, 'We are all Republicans, we are all
Federalists.' It had 'a wonderful lullaby effect' on the jumpy
country.

The America that Jefferson serenely planned to put back on
'her republican tack' was a land of five million people, mostly
farm folk; nearly one-fifth Negro slaves. Britain at this time
had fifteen million, and France twenty-five million people.

More than two-thirds of the population lived within fifty
miles of the Atlantic. Down the centre of the country ran a
great spine of mountains, at least 100 miles wide. It divided
the eastern from the frontier states. By 1800 there were three
new States in the Union: Vermont, Kentucky and Tennessee.

America was still a country of enormous forests. When Mrs
Adams journeyed to Washington she said, 'Woods are all you

American farm

see from Baltimore until you reach the city.' A traveller through upper New York State described lonely cabins in deep woods, their yards hardly scratched for corn and potatoes. He saw a well-dressed woman with white hands feeding her chickens. The traveller knew if he came back in three years he would find a fine house and cultivated fields.

The combined population of the five biggest cities came to only 180,000. Philadelphia, the leading city, had schools, hospitals, bookstores, print shops and a harbour full of ships. But like New York it was swept with frequent epidemics. In 1793 when a severe yellow fever epidemic sent the government fleeing to nearby Germantown, three future presidents, Jefferson, Madison and James Monroe, had to share one bedroom and two beds!

72

Washington, D.C., the brand-new capital, was built on swamp and red clay. It had eight boarding houses, an oyster house, a tavern, workmen's shacks, a few stores and the half-built White House, a muddy mile and a half away from the half-built Capitol.

Communication and transportation were by far the greatest problems. On his trip from his home in Virginia to Washington, Jefferson had to cross eight rivers: 'Five have neither bridges nor boats.' A 150-mile sail up the Hudson River could take from three days to two weeks, depending on the wind.

But Americans were fiercely proud of their new Republic, chopped out of a forest. Even friendly French travellers complained they were 'stinking with national conceit', and 'thought nothing is good and that no one has any brains except Americans'. Symbolic of this spirit is the change made in American spelling at this time. Noah Webster, a New England journalist, wrote the 'American Spelling Book' and a dictionary (still used) which established differences between American and British spelling that persist today. 'America', he declared, 'must be as independent in literature as she is in politics, as famous for arts as for arms.'

As a sign that he meant to do away with the 'pomp and state' of Washington and Adams, Jefferson rode alone on horseback to his inauguration and tethered his horse himself to the fence. To show Republican simplicity he lounged about the White House in old clothes—although his dinner parties were delicious, with sparkling talk and wine. One critic said: 'I wish his French politics were as good as his French wines.' But his rule of pell-mell instead of ceremony at diplomatic functions infuriated his gold-braided foreign guests and their wives.

Besides Republican simplicity Jefferson demanded thrift. To help him give America a 'wise and frugal government' he chose his old friend, James Madison, for Secretary of State, and the Swiss-born financier, Albert Gallatin, to be Secretary of the Treasury. 'Three more agreeable men were never collected around the dinner-table of the White House.'

Jefferson required strict economy. The national debt dropped from 83 to 57 million dollars while he was President. Jefferson believed 'the earth belongs to the living generation' who shouldn't have to pay heavy taxes because of their ancestors' extravagance. Although his enemies had called him a dangerous radical and atheist, Jefferson was neither. He did not change the solid financial system Hamilton had begun. The national bank and Mint had worked well for twelve years; he did not disturb them.

Jefferson had promised that no one would lose a political job just because he was a Federalist. Adams made this a hard promise to keep. The night before he left the Presidency, Adams had sat up late signing appointments of fifteen judges —to lifetime judgeships. They were all diehard Federalists. These 'midnight appointments' infuriated Jefferson. The posts, he felt, should have been left empty for him to give to his followers.

His foreign policy followed that of Washington and Adams. America should make money by trading with warring England and France but not become otherwise involved in the strife. Like Washington, and unlike Adams, he was keenly interested in the western frontier, its welfare and future. His greatest achievements as President involved the West.

In 1801 Jefferson learned to his dismay that the year before, by secret treaty, easy-going Spain had ceded all of Louisiana to imperialist France. He said grimly: 'The day France takes possession of New Orleans, we must marry ourselves to the British fleet and Nation.' He ordered Robert Livingston, his envoy in Paris, to find out if France would sell New Orleans and West Florida to America for $10 million.

By now Napoleon, master of most of Europe, dreamt of regaining France's lost American empire. He shipped a French army to the French-owned island of Haiti in the Caribbean. With Haiti as a base he planned to move on to Louisiana. While Napoleon planned a French empire in Louisiana, Jefferson was pondering a project of his own: what he called a 'literary expedition' through Louisiana, up the Missouri River,

74

Map 6—*United States after the Louisiana Purchase*

down the Columbia and to the Pacific Coast.

To head it he chose his young secretary, a fellow-Virginian, tall, twenty-seven-year old Meriwether Lewis. Lewis was an Army veteran and a skilled map-maker. For a year he and the widower, Jefferson, lived in the barnlike White House, as lonely, Jefferson said, 'as two mice in a church'. Together they studied botany, astronomy, geology, Indian history and languages, preparing for Jefferson's 'darling project'.

While Jefferson and Lewis prepared for the 'darling project.' Napoleon's dream of an empire in America died. His French army of 37,000 was destroyed by Negro uprisings and yellow fever as soon as it touched Haiti. Napoleon knew he couldn't hold Louisiana against the British navy without a base in Haiti. Rather than have England seize it, he decided to sell Louisiana to the United States.

So when Livingston called on Napoleon's foreign minister, Talleyrand, to ask how much France would take for New Orleans and West Florida he was astounded to have Talleyrand ask, 'Would the United States wish to have the whole of Louisiana?' As the startled American fumbled for a reply, the French diplomat pressed on, 'What would you give for the whole of Louisiana?'

Negotiotions began and in May 1803, Louisiana's nine million uncharted square miles went to the United States for less than $15 million. The country had doubled in size. As Talleyrand said: 'You have made a noble bargain for yourselves.'

The frontiersmen were overjoyed at this huge extension to their territory and a free passage up and down the Mississippi River to New Orleans, their trade lifeline. But the prospect of big, new western states with needs and interests far different from their own, unnerved many easterners. Massachusetts' Fisher Ames lamented that the Louisiana Purchase would send the country 'rushing like a comet into infinite space'. Some New England Federalists plotted to join their States to Canada, rather than be dominated by the big, new West.

76   By now Meriwether Lewis and another Army officer, genial

William Clark, had set out on their two-year, four-month 'literary expedition' exploring the way west. They led forty-three 'healthy, unmarried men accustomed to the woods', an Indian guide, Sacajawea or Bird Woman, and a 160-pound dog. Their gear included twenty-four tomahawks, scalping knives, thirty gallons of whisky and Dr Rush's bilious pills. When they returned safely in September 1806 they had com-

Lewis and Clark confer with friendly Indians

pleted one of the great scientific expeditions of all time and brought back the first complete picture of the American West —as well as prehistoric bones, two grizzly bear cubs, strange minerals, seeds Jefferson planted in his garden, and a Mandan Indian Chief and his wife whom Jefferson entertained at the White House.

In 1804, Jefferson was re-elected President. He carried all the States except Connecticut and Delaware—the greatest presidential victory until Franklin Roosevelt's landslide in 1936. He began his second term in the White House a success-ful diplomat and serene scholar with a lively curiosity and cultivated mind—a happy man and President.

14 Exiles and Slaves

The Tories with their brats and wives
Have fled to save their wretched lives.

For two groups of Americans the young Republic held small hope of the 'blessings of liberty' promised by the Constitution.

One was the Loyalists—or as their enemies called them, the Tories. The flight of the Tories (Americans who chose to remain faithful to England rather than join the Revolution) began with the war and continued when it was over. The most politically important Tories settled in Canada.

Before 1783 more than 3,000 Loyalists settled in the province of Nova Scotia. After 1783, 30,000 more followed. Three Canadian provinces were developed by these refugees— Nova Scotia, New Brunswick and Prince Edward Island. Among them were leading New Yorkers like Sir John Johnson and Colonel James DeLancey. The Chief Justice and half the graduates of Harvard came from Massachusetts—bringing the Royal Coat of Arms from the Boston Council Chamber with them. It still hangs in an Anglican church in New Brunswick.

The British government gave the Tories over £6 million, ranging from £45,000, to the great Mohawk Valley land-owner, Sir John Johnson, to £10 or £12 to Army privates. It gave them cattle, pigs, seed, tools and, for three years, rations of flour, pork and beef. The refugees soon learned to add beaver tails and buffalo tongues to this diet. Tragically, the fourth year of exile was one of drought and poor crops.

Many Tories starved to death in the Hungry Year of 1788.

The Tories had a harsh, pioneering life. They could bring almost nothing from their homes in America on the jam-packed refugee ships or up the wilderness trails. Soldiers' families were sheltered in big army tents until cabins were built. The first cabins were 20-feet long, or less, had a hole in the roof for smoke, hard dirt floors, and oiled paper in the windows. When better homes were built these first cabins became pig sties.

Tories camp on a Canadian river bank

The Tories travelled up-river in flat boats. Each family had a location ticket. When they reached their location, lots were drawn. The lots closest to the river were the best. Majors or higher got 5,000 acres; captains, 3,000; subalterns, 2,000; privates, 200.

The Tories worked together on everything. A man by himself could clear an acre in a week; six men together could do it in a day. Together they built houses, barns and villages; butchered pigs and cattle; ploughed, hauled and harvested; even peeled and strung pumpkins. These community activities were called 'bees' and were good excuses for parties, too. A hundred men could build a barn in one day. They divided into two teams and raced to see which side went up first.

By 1800 most of the American laws against the Tories had been repealed. Men like Hamilton wanted the Tories to come 79 home. They said, 'We have already lost too large a number of valuable citizens.' Many homesick Tories did go back to America. Those who stayed changed Canadian history.

First, they gave Canada a large English-speaking population. Until now Canada had been mostly French. Second, though loyal to the Crown, they brought 'their cursed Republican town-meeting spirit' with them and demanded that their traditional legal rights as Englishmen be recognised.

Both the British Prime Minister, William Pitt, and the Governor-in-Chief of British North America, Lord Dorchester, saw that their claim was just. In 1791, less than ten years after the defeat at Yorktown, the Canada Act went through Parliament. It gave Canada a start toward a kind of representative government which developed and spread all over the British Empire, and provided the political foundations for a newer, larger empire than the thirteen lost American colonies.

If the lot of the American Tories grew better, the condition of another group of Americans, the Negro slaves, grew worse.

American whites in both North and South were slave-owners; Hamilton, as well as Jefferson and Washington. Right after the Revolution there was a strong movement to free the slaves. Anti-slavery societies, mostly religious in origin, spread. In the 1780s State after northern State banned slavery. But in the 1790s the cotton gin was invented—a machine for taking the seeds out of cotton. This brought wealth to both southern planters and northern millowners. Between 1790 and 1808 more than 100,000 Negroes were carried to America on slave ships to pick southern cotton for northern and British mills to spin.

Some Negroes tried to help themselves. American Negro churches provided the little social and community life allowed the slaves. Slave rebels led bloody uprisings on the plantations. These uprisings terrified the white owners. After each one the laws governing slaves became harsher and their life less free.

Above: *Halifax—haven for American Tories in Canada. They said that they sailed for Hell, Hull (England) or Halifax (Canada)*

Below: *The Spotswood Payne children with their nurse*

Despite increasing obstacles some free Negroes made their mark. Among them were the New Orleans doctor, James Derham, and Richard Allen, founder of the first American Negro Church (The African Methodist Episcopal Church). Best known, perhaps, are Benjamin Banneker, the astronomer, and the poet, Phillis Wheatley.

Banneker was born free in Maryland. He educated himself in astronomy and mathematics, made the first American clock, and edited an almanac. He is famous for work on the commission that laid out Washington. When the French engineer who headed it, Major Pierre L'Enfant, left America with the job half-done, Banneker, who had a remarkable memory, reproduced the city plans. When his long and useful life ended in 1806, a Baltimore, Maryland, newspaper wrote; 'He was known in the neighbourhood for his quiet and peaceful *demeanour* and among scientific men as an astronomer and mathematician.'

Phillis Wheatley came as a child from Senegal in Africa. She was bought, educated and freed by a Boston Quaker family. In 1770 her first poem was printed. Her verse became world-famous, admired by both Washington and Voltaire. She wrote religious poetry and translated the Latin poet, Ovid. A disastrous marriage wrecked her life. She was a cleaning woman in a Boston boarding house when she died at thirty.

How did Franklin, Washington, Adams, Jefferson—men who in 1776 declared 'all men are created free and equal'—look at slavery? With guilt, concern and foreboding. But slaves were the greatest source of national wealth. During the Constitutional Convention in 1787, the 569 slaves owned by the four delegates from South Carolina were worth half as much again as all the public securities of all the other delegates!

Franklin's last political act was to sign a petition to abolish slavery. This so enraged some slave-holding senators that they prevented official mourning after his death. Washington wrote in 1786: 'There is not a man living who wishes more sincerely than I do to see a plan adopted for the abolition of slavery.'

(Under his will, all his slaves were freed after his widow died.) Mrs Adams once reminded her husband: 'To fight for liberty and deny that blessing to others is wicked.' The last law Jefferson signed as President made the slave trade piracy, and death its punishment. (The British Government banned the slave trade the same year.) Of slavery Jefferson once said: 'I tremble for my country when I reflect that God is just.'

15   Jefferson at Bay

Jefferson's second term as President began in March 1805. It was as troubled as his first had been triumphant. One cause of trouble was Aaron Burr, no longer Vice President, and a bitter, ruined man.

When in 1801 Hamilton engineered Jefferson's defeat of Burr, and then blocked Burr's election as Governor of New York soon after, he signed his own death warrant. When Burr heard that Hamilton had said he 'was a dangerous man who ought not to be trusted with the reins of government', he challenged him to a duel. At dawn on 11 July 1804, on the banks of the Hudson River, the Vice President of the United States fatally shot the former Secretary of the Treasury, making a national martyr of a man to whom the early Republic owed its strength, but who shortly before his death said sadly, 'Every day proves to me more and more that this American world was not made for me.' Hamilton had made Jefferson President; Jefferson was fashioning an America Hamilton intensely disapproved of. Burr was indicted for murder in one State, a fugitive in two more.

Jobless and bankrupt, Burr, like Napoleon, began to dream of empire. No one knows for sure whether he meant to carve it out of the American frontier or Mexico across the border. He first tried England for help. He was refused. He approached the Spanish and then several disgruntled frontier generals. One, James Wilkinson, first agreed to aid him, then, having second thoughts, wrote to Jefferson of Burr's 'deep, dark, wicked and wide conspiracy'.

At first Jefferson didn't believe the rumours of Burr's plots.

Finally, he ordered Burr's arrest. Burr was captured and carried for trial to the beautiful House of Delegates in Richmond, Virginia, that Jefferson had designed. Burr was lucky. The judge (because he was the judge of the Virginia circuit court as well as Chief Justice of the Supreme Court) was John Marshall, Jefferson's third cousin.

In January 1801, a few months before John Adams left the presidency, he had made John Marshall, Chief Justice of the Supreme Court. Marshall, like Adams, was a confirmed Federalist. He said that so far as he was concerned Republicans were 'divided into speculative theorists and absolute terrorists. With the latter I am disposed to class Mr Jefferson.' As Chief Justice, the tall, black-eyed, black-haired Marshall had sworn in his tall red-headed cousin as President. For the next eight years the Federalist Marshall did his conscientious best to keep Jefferson from putting America back 'on her Republican tack'. (Jefferson called his cousin John, 'a crafty chief judge'.)

To Jefferson's fury the jury returned the verdict, 'Not proved' and Aaron Burr went free. Burr left the country, but years later came back, married a rich old widow, and lived in a handsome house called the Jumel Mansion, still standing in New York City.

For thirty years John Marshall was Chief Justice of the Supreme Court. Jefferson was President only eight. Marshall made the United States Supreme Court, despite ups and downs, almost all-powerful. He championed individual against majority rights, rights of property, the Federal over the State governments. Above all he established the Supreme Court's power to declare a law unconstitutional and therefore *void*. Since Marshall, the Supreme Court has been a legal umpire, and the stumbling block in the road of many a masterful President. The old Federalist, John Adams, said in 1826 'my gift of John Marshall to the people of the United States is the proudest act of my life', and Justice Oliver Wendell Holmes wrote seventy-five years later: 'If American law were to be represented by a single figure, the figure could be one alone, and that one, John Marshall.'

John Marshall, Chief Justice of the Supreme Court, who gave the Court its great power

But separatist movements and stiff-necked judges at home did not bring real disaster to Jefferson. This came through trouble with England and France.

England and France had been locked in deadly warfare since 1793—almost fifteen years—with enormous losses in men, land and ships. One of their chief weapons against each other was sea blockade. After the Battle of Trafalgar in 1805 England ruled the waves. To get men for their battered and all-important Navy, the British kept stopping American ships and taking off crewmen. In 1807 Madison proposed at a Cabinet meeting that if Britain promised to give up impressing sailors America might return to her all the British sailors who had been on American ships less than two years. When Gallatin pointed out it would cost America 5,000 seamen, the deal was never offered to the British government.

The British Navy by now was blockading the very mouth of New York Harbour, stopping and searching American ships within ten miles of the American coast. When in 1807 (during the Burr crisis) a British man o' war halted the 'Chesapeake' and fired on her because the American ship refused to be searched, the United States was angry enough to go to war. 'Never', wrote Jefferson, 'since the Battle of Lexington have I seen this country in such a state of *exasperation*.'

To save money, Jefferson had reduced both the Army and the Navy so drastically that America was too weak to do anything but complain, protest, and demand apologies—and order all foreign ships out of American waters. England ignored America's orders; so did France. Napoleon called the American flag 'a piece of striped bunting'. Since America was too weak to fight, what could Jefferson use as a 'substitute for war or submission'?

His solution was an economic one, an *embargo*. Three days before Christmas in 1807 'to keep our seamen and property from capture and to starve the offending nations' he forbade any American ship to sail into foreign waters. Jefferson thought England and France were more dependent on American goods and food than they really were. It was no use. As an English Admiralty lawyer said, if 'our ships of war are in want of men while Englishmen are to be found in numbers on board American ships, we always fall upon some good excuse for impressing His Majesty's *liege* subjects, find them there where we may'.

If the British had small respect for Jefferson's embargo, many Americans had less. Since they couldn't ship their goods openly, they smuggled. Throughout the blockade, even when they had lost two out of three ships to France or England the profits on the one that got through more than made up the difference. But smuggling was no substitute for world trade. In one year American exports dropped from $110 million to $20 million. In five months there were 125 bankruptcies in New York City alone. Virginia farmers suffered as much as New England merchants. They had no market for their cotton and tobacco. The embargo ruined Jefferson among others.

The OGRABME (Embargo spelled backwards). In this Federalist cartoon the OGRABME bites an American merchant who is trying to smuggle tobacco into a ship. The OGRABME was often represented as a turtle.

An English visitor described New York Harbour: 'Not a

bale, box, cask, barrel, or package was to be seen. The streets near the waterside were almost deserted, the grass had begun to grow on the wharves.' Small seaports like New Haven, Connecticut, as well as great ones like Salem, Massachusetts, suffered losses from which they never recovered.

From all over America, Jefferson received abuse. 'You infernal villain,' one letter said, 'how much longer are you going to keep this damn embargo to starve us?' New England and New York merchants smuggled into Canada. Open rebellion broke out in Vermont, and Jefferson sent troops to 'crush these *audacious* proceedings'.

Dismayed at the suffering the embargo was causing, Jefferson reversed his ideas on the question of American business and manufacturing. He began to encourage factories and mills, industry and banks. He realised, as Hamilton had, that America could not survive just as a farming country.

But it was no use. During his last half year in office, Jefferson became a 'more odious President, even to the Republicans, than John Adams'. But still he believed that an embargo could be a great weapon as a substitute for war. It deserved a 'fair experiment' and he refused to remove it. Years later he still protested: 'If we had suffered our vessels, cargoes and seamen to have gone out, all would have been taken by England or its enemies, and America gone to war'.

At last, three days before he left office in March 1809, he gave in to the farmers, businessmen, congressmen and his own Cabinet. He repealed 'the miserable and mischievous failure', the embargo. He was terribly disappointed at the failure of his 'fair experiment' at peace-keeping. As he wrote to an old friend: 'Never did a prisoner released from his chains feel such relief as I shall on shaking off the *shackles* of power.'

His Secretary of State and fellow-Virginian, James Madison, succeeded him as President on 4 March. On 11 March Jefferson went home to his farm, Monticello, and, safe in port, he never left Virginia again.

16   Man of Monticello

'All my wishes end where I hope my days will end, at Monticello.' In March 1809 Jefferson left the 'splendid misery' of
the White House for his Virginia home and his hobbies. His
home was Monticello, a red brick mansion on a mountain
top near Charlottesville. It is one of the most beautiful houses
in the world. His hobbies were architecture; farming—he
pioneered crop rotation and *soil conservation*; languages—he
read French, Italian, Spanish, Latin, Greek and Anglo-
Saxon. He was a lifelong scientist, especially interested in
paleontology, *ethnology* and botany. He was the inventor
(among other things) of the decimal money system, a violinist
and composer.

Jefferson had one of the liveliest and widest-ranging minds
in history. In 1962 when President John Kennedy greeted a
group of Nobel Prize winners he said they were 'the most
extraordinary collection of talent, of human knowledge, that
has ever been gathered in the White House with the possible
exception of when Thomas Jefferson dined alone'.

'Architecture', Jefferson said, 'is my delight and putting up
and pulling down one of my favourite amusements.' As a
young man in Europe he sat entranced for hours by the
Maison Carrée in southern France, 'gazing like a lover at his
mistress'. He designed courthouses, churches, his friends'
homes, and in his old age, the University of Virginia. (He
submitted a design, anonymously, for the White House.)
He spoke of God as the Divine Architect.

Monticello was his masterpiece. He began it before his
marriage. While it was still a one-room cottage he brought

Monticello, Jefferson's home in Virginia

his bride to it through the snow. This small, square honeymoon cottage stands at the end of one of the two long wings which reach forward in a great U from the columned and domed centre house. Jefferson imported Italian craftsmen to carve its fireplaces, mould stars and eagles for its ceilings, and lay *parquet* floors of his design. He filled his home with his inventions: a seven-day calendar clock on pulleys that hang through the floor of the entrance hall down into the cellar; a bed that disappears into the ceiling; doors that open and close on springs; a dumb-waiter; a swivel chair; a new kind of plough and wheelbarrow. His library of 6,000 books held a first edition of Milton's 'Paradise Lost', a black-letter Chaucer, the 'Anglo-Saxon Chronicle'. One-quarter of his books were in foreign languages. There was one cookery book. Monticello had trophies from Lewis and Clark's expedition, fine furniture bought in Paris and London, marble busts of his old friends, Franklin, Washington, Lafayette and John Paul Jones.

Jefferson's bed stood in an alcove between his bedroom and study. Elk and moose antlers, brought home by Lewis and Clark, and a calendar clock hung in the front hall of Monticello

Once home, Jefferson never went more than a hundred miles away. But his letters travelled all over the world. He received more than 1,200 a year. Eight to thirty-seven guests dined with him daily, and drank from silver cups marked 'G.W. to T.J.'

Widowed young, he adored his daughters and grand-children. His younger daughter, Polly, was dead, but the elder, Martha Jefferson Randolph, and her big family lived with him. He had missed them terribly in Washington.

Lack of money was his great worry. Jefferson was one of the many farmers whom the embargo ruined. He was so hospit-able (and could never resist new books, or ornaments to make Monticello more beautiful) that he sank deeper and deeper into debt. Since, as he said, 'land in this State cannot now be sold for a month's rent', he could not raise any money. (Monticello was sold soon after his death to pay his debts.) But his old age was made happy by his renewed friendship with John Adams, and his fulfilled dream, the University of Virginia.

Adams and Jefferson had been close friends when they were young. As Adams wrote, Jefferson 'soon seized on my heart'. They had worked together in the First Continental Congress. Adams chose Jefferson to write the Declaration of Indepen-dence. They had been diplomats together in Europe. Mrs Adams had taken care of Jefferson's motherless little girl, Polly, in London. In Paris John Quincy Adams had been, as the father reminded Jefferson when the son became American President in 1825, 'almost as much your boy as mine'.

But the bad blood between the Federalists and Republicans gradually estranged them. Adams was hurt and angered by the campaign Jefferson waged against him in 1800; Jefferson, enraged by Adams' 'midnight appointments'. For twelve years after that they had nothing to do with each other.

By 1811 their good old friend Dr Benjamin Rush was determined they should become friends again. He made him-self their go-between. At first neither responded. But when Jefferson was told that Adams had said 'I always loved

The University of Virginia fulfilled one of Jefferson's dreams

Jefferson and still love him', and Adams learned Jefferson's reaction, 'This is enough for me, I knew him always to be an honest man and often a great one', on New Year's day, 1812, Adams wrote Jefferson a friendly note. Jefferson replied at once: 'We were fellow labourers in the same cause, struggling for what is most valuable to man, his right of self-government.'

For the next fourteen years a stream of letters crossed the 500 miles between Monticello and Quincy, Massachusetts. Adams wrote three to Jefferson's one. They discussed books, science, old friends and enemies, history, religion, government, the Greek philosophers and Genghis Khan. As Adams said, 'You and I ought not to die until we have explained ourselves to each other.' They never wrote on politics. Jefferson would not do it. 'Where there are so many subjects on which we agree, why should we introduce the only one on which we differ?' he asked.

Jefferson's other great satisfaction was the University of Virginia. Jefferson felt universal education was vital to a democracy. It was the only way 'every man can judge for himself what will secure or endanger his freedom'. All his life Jefferson had wanted Virginia to build a good university, so that her young men need not travel North or to Europe to study.

At last, in 1818, plans were made for a university to be built on 200 acres in Charlottesville, Virginia, in the valley right below Monticello. Jefferson made a design based on his favourite Château de Marly in France. There were arcades and colonnades linked by small pavilions; enclosed gardens behind them; a great rotunda set high on steps at the head. Before the digging started Jefferson crawled all through the vines and bushes measuring. While its buildings were going up Jefferson, in his seventies and still 'straight as a gun barrel', daily rode down on horseback to check its progress. He peered at it through a spy glass in his library in bad weather. His overseer said 'He took as much pains seeing everything done right as if it had been his own house.'

Jefferson wrote all over Europe urging outstanding teachers to come to Charlottesville; served as the University's first Rector; welcomed both teachers and students to Monticello.

Though he never left Virginia he knew and cared about everything happening in the United States. A great new road connected Cumberland on the Potomac to St Louis on the Mississippi; a canal was cut linking New York City to the Great Lakes. There was a second war and peace with England; more quarrels with the Indians. Florida was bought from Spain for $1 million; the border disagreement between America and Canada was settled peacefully. Steamboats puffed from New Orleans to Pittsburgh, and in 1819 crossed the Atlantic. The population topped 10 million, and more than a quarter of them lived in the West. There were seven new states in the Union—and seven new stars in the American flag. And under his friends, Presidents Madison and James Monroe, America stayed 'on her Republican tack'.

By 1826 Thomas Jefferson was in his mid-eighties; Adams, ninety years old. The Fourth of July 1826 would be the fiftieth Anniversary of the Declaration of Independence. As the great day drew near, their countrymen wanted to bring the two old patriots together. By now both were ill and feeble, Adams almost blind. A nine-day journey separated them. It

The Fourth of July has always been a great American holiday. Here is an 1816 Fourth of July celebration

was impossible, although Jefferson had written to Adams: 'We shall meet again and so believes your friend, and if we are disappointed we shall never know it.'

Both men longed to live until the Fourth of July, their country's fiftieth birthday. They got their wish. Adams died at six o'clock on the afternoon of the Fourth. His last words were, 'Thomas Jefferson still lives.' He could not know that his old friend had died six hours before him.

Adams was buried under a seventeen-line epitaph composed by his son, President John Quincy Adams—not the simple phrase he had wanted on how he had kept the peace with France in 1800. Jefferson had told his daughter what he wanted cut on his gravestone. He wanted to be remembered for the Declaration of Independence, the Statute of Virginia for Religious Freedom, and the University of Virginia—the three great causes of his life: civil liberty, religious liberty and universal education.

George Washington started America safely on her way. Hamilton made her government strong. But to Thomas Jefferson we owe our hopes and dreams.

HOW DO WE KNOW?

When George Washington, Alexander Hamilton or Thomas Jefferson wanted to talk to people they had no telephone or telegraph to help them. So they wrote letters. Such letters, diaries and newspaper articles are the basis for much in this book.

But I wanted to give the background for these 18th century letters and diaries. I wanted to show how people lived in the young republic, how Indian attacks on the West and the French Revolution in Europe changed their lives. I read many books on these subjects.

I saw many places also. Washington's home, Mount Vernon, still stands. So does Jefferson's beautiful Monticello. There is Independence Hall in Philadelphia and the white houses built by Salem sea captains. I visited these places while I was writing this book. Someday I hope you can see them too. They will tell you better than any book about life in the young American republic.

THINGS TO DO

1. Write and act a scene about either George Washington or Thomas Jefferson at home.
2. Write a story about Americans moving westward and Indians attacking them. You could illustrate your story with pictures.
3. What is meant by 'a hoop for the barrel' (p. 25)? Discuss in class why it was so difficult to find a strong enough one.
4. Turn the class into a meeting of the delegates in Independence Hall 1787. Hold a debate on the slavery question.
5. Write a list of all the chief differences between the British and the United States Constitutions which you can find.
6. What does the Stars and Stripes tell us about the United States?
7. Paint a picture of George Washington arriving in New York to be made the first president of the United States.
8. Write descriptions of Alexander Hamilton and Thomas Jefferson so as to show why they stood in opposition to each other.
9. Read the book in this series on the French Revolution. Discuss what is meant on p. 56 by saying that the French Revolution 'drew a red-hot ploughshare through American history'.
10. Imagine you were the captain who survived the ambush set by the Indian Chief Little Turtle (p. 53). Write the story of your terrible adventure.
11. Hold a class debate on which of the first three presidents did the most for the United States.

GLOSSARY

adjourn, put off to another day
anarchy, disorder arising from lack of government
ancestral, inherited from forefathers
audacious, bold
canebrake, thick growth of cane
combustibles, anything that will burn (Washington was likening rebellion to fire)
contending, fighting
counterfeiters, makers of imitation coins or notes of money
crop rotation, practice of planting different crops in turn to avoid exhausting the soil
demeanour, behaviour
demoniacal, devilish, diabolical
diplomat, one who represents his country abroad
disinterested, free of self-interest
dissension, disagreement
dotage, feebleness of mind caused by old age
doubloons, old Spanish gold coins
ducats, gold coins common on the Continent in past centuries
ecclesiastical, associated with church matters
embargo, ban on trade
encroachment, intrusion on someone else's ground
ethnology, knowledge of different human races
etiquette, rules of society or good manners
exasperation, annoyance caused by repeated irritation
executive, the part of the government or business which carries out laws, plans or policies
formidable, difficult (or alarming), to oppose
gallant, dashing young man (pronounced gall*ant*)
habeas corpus, (Latin, 'have the body'), a rule of law by which an accused man must be brought to court and just reason be given for his arrest
harmonize, be in agreement

hemlock, coniferous evergreen tree

impeachment, accusation by the government of serious offences

infernal, hellish

judicial, concerned with interpretation of the law

legislative, concerned with making laws

levee, official party

liege, free but owing service, duty

moidores, old Portuguese gold coins

nankeen, cotton cloth

naturalisation, legal process by which a foreign person becomes a citizen of another country

navigable, usable by ships

neutrality, position of not taking sides

paleontology, knowledge of fossils in the earth

parquet, polished wood blocks used in floors

patent, letter giving official backing to the holder

pieces of eight, old Spanish dollars

precedent, a happening which may be used as an example allowing it to happen again; a legal guide to future actions

predicted, foretold

privateer, armed ship privately owned but licensed by government to attack enemy ships

prostrated, laid low

puissant, powerful

quorum, agreed number of people who must be present before a meeting can make effective decisions

ratify, confirm, give official consent to

reprieve, delay in execution of a sentence or to set free

satellite, hanger-on, a person (country or planet) dependent on another who is greater or more powerful

secular, not connected with the church

shackles, something which restricts freedom of movement

sloop, a single-masted sailing vessel

soil conservation, action taken to prevent soil being used in such a way that it is worn away or made infertile

supercilious, contemptuous

tranquillity, quietness

typhoon, violent wind

veteran, one with long experience of war or military life

vitals, interior part of the body essential to life

void, empty, worthless, having no legal force